Signed as below.

12 —

11024/19.95
205

For Sylvia & Charles

With regards and shared
experiences these last two years!

Norman

The Journal Men

The Journal Men

P.D. Ross, E. Norman Smith and Grattan O'Leary of *The Ottawa Journal:* Three Great Canadian Newspapermen and the Tradition They Created

By I. Norman Smith

McClelland and Stewart Limited

McClelland and Stewart Limited
The Canadian Publishers
25 Hollinger Road, Toronto

To Fran, without whom...

Acknowledgements

I am grateful to Grattan O'Leary, Tom Lowrey and Howard Ross for their lively recollections, though they share no blame for the text, for they haven't seen it! I was fortunate to be able to draw on two fine books: *The Canadian Press* (Ryerson) by M. E. Nichols; and *News and the Southams* (Macmillan) by Charles Bruce. Gil Purcell, John Dauphinee and Betty Shewan (librarian) of the Canadian Press kept me straight on CP here and there, but they too are blame-free for faults. Irma Coucill's sketches of The Journal Men support the cliché that a picture is worth a thousand words.

I.N.S.

Contents

Introduction

A friend once told me of his two-year-old son pointing to a bureau and asking what it was. On being told it was a bureau the boy asked: "What's it doing?" Bill didn't find that an easy question to answer.

This is a book, I believe, but what's it doing?

It is something of a biography of three great Canadian journalists: P.D. Ross, E. Norman Smith, and M. Grattan O'Leary. I say "something of a biography" for it touches mostly on the aspects of their lives and characters that made them outstanding journalists.

I am aware, too, that it lacks the impartiality that attends good biography. As I worked for and then with them from 1928 through 1972, as I learned and tried to extend their influence into my own times, I am not inclined to find much fault with what they were doing. Criticism makes for gaiety and mischief, and good reading. But as I followed them as president and editor of *The Ottawa Journal*, and as one was my father and all were my friends it is just "not on" that I play Smart Alec.

What am I doing here, then? I am setting down for the record what these men did and stood for. I place them in their times without arguing with them from ours. In these days of instant opinion and instanter rebuttal, my approach may seem negative. But is it? I remember the impact on me of Arthur Miller's demanding line in *Death of a Salesman*: "Attention must be paid." History does not begin with the views of my generation, nor experience.

As will be seen, I am not a biographer. I can try to write only as a reporter—a high objective if we think of such as Grant Dexter, Ken Wilson, Blair Fraser, James Reston, Ross Munro's war despatches, Matt Halton's broadcasts from Europe. I believe that Ross, Smith and O'Leary are worth reporting, and the less I get in the way the better. Here and there I will slip in some of my own thoughts after 44 years in journalism, but they won't be cluttersome.

What did Ross do with *The Journal* after he bought half of it for $4,000 in 1886? What were the problems, in 1917, of creating The Canadian Press, in which Smith took a major part? What endowed O'Leary's emotional conviction that freedom of the press was no more than man's individual freedom of speech? I try to answer such questions.

There are lots of quotes in this book, and quite a variety. Ross tells of John A. Macdonald in his cups, stoutly defends French Canadians, and recalls, with remorse, killing a moose. Smith leads the fight for cooperative exchange of world news, insists that if a press is to be free it must be responsible, muses on why he put down his violin for his pen as a career. O'Leary defines what religion means to him, relishes the ecstacies of political joy and anger, and describes the sinking of the *Titanic*.

I tell of their youth: of Ross the champion athlete, Smith a short-hand cub reporter in Fleet Street, O'Leary on a poor farm by the sea. I show them in their office, zealous for principle but making room for laughter, and how age held no fear nor much change for any of them.

Is it better not to write at all on a deserving theme than to do it inadequately? Certainly silence would have been easier. But I imagined I had a duty to get it down for the record. No one was as close as I was to all three of these lives—daily, professionally and personally.

Ross and my father wrote no "life story." I have for years been urging O'Leary to write his, but his still very active and useful life has made that task easy to put off. "It's a hell of a job, Norman." In the meantime he urged me to go ahead with my idea of a three-vista memoir, giving me several lively recollections. God willing, we will yet get from him the force, gaiety and dedication to life he himself would write.

This is not a history of *The Journal*, but a look at the three men who made it, and who, I believe, were leaders in shaping a responsible role for journalism in Canadian democracy.

P.D. Ross

Philip Dansken Ross was born in Montreal, January 1, 1858, nine years before Confederation. Canada's population was then about 3,100,000. When he first became a reporter the Dominion was only eleven years old, still a child of England. Its total expenditures were $30,000,000, its revenues $22,000,000. When he died, July 5, 1949, Canada had been through three major wars. Its population was 13,450,000, its expenditures $2,200,000,000 against revenues of $2,775,000,000. When he was nine there were four provinces: when he died there were nine, with Newfoundland still to come. Canada had become independent of the old British Empire, the new Commonwealth and the Mother Country. Canada strode in seven league boots in P.D. Ross' ninety-one-and-a-half years, and so did P.D. Ross, enjoying every mile and minute of it.

He was, I believe, a great Canadian, a great journalist. He was 51 years older than I; yet from 1928 when I began to work with The Ottawa Journal until his death in 1949 he was always thoughtful of us all, inspiring, and, with awesome brevity, instructive.

Mr. Ross lived but did not write his life story. As I was "there", so to speak, in the shop with him and witness to how he thought, worked and lived, I want to set down something of that story—aided by the recollection of his relatives and friends and some patient digging into such letters, documents and writings as remain.

Setting Out in Seven League Boots . . .

The story in Canada opens with his father Philip Simpson Ross, who emigrated from Forth, Scotland, in 1853. He had been born in Belfast, Ireland, in 1827. His father, a Scotsman, was in Ireland serving on military duty. After doing odd jobs in Upper and Lower Canada, P.S. Ross, who had had some experience in the ship provision business in Scotland, set up a small ship chandlery on Grey Nuns street, by the Montreal Harbor. The short street is still there, dominated by the backs of large warehouses. It was in rooms over that shop that P.D. Ross was born.

At 29, Philip S. Ross wrote home to his church minister in Scotland, giving him the names of three ladies with whom he was acquainted and asking the minister to enquire whether any of them would marry him. It is joked in the family that the first two who were asked, declined. The third, Christina Chalmers Dansken, aged 26, of Glasgow, took the sailboat to Portland, Mass., where she was met by her letter-writing friend. They married then and there in Portland, December 10, 1856.

On a river frozen nearly half the year the chandlery business was not likely to be any great success. On May 1, 1858, Ross sent out notices he would do invoices and pass goods through customs, and take care of people's accounts. That idea was a winner. He had earlier sent for his two brothers, James and William, to come out from Scotland to join him in the ship provision business. Now he himself set up a reputation in accounting that led to the first association of accountancy in Montreal and Quebec, following only by a shade the Institute of Chartered Accountants of Scotland, founded in 1853 and the first of its kind in the world. P.S. Ross and Sons might be the oldest surviving accounting firm in the world. In 1976 it will have done the Sun Life for a hundred years. It has done the Bell Telephone audit for 96 or 97 years. (In 1958 P.S. Ross and Sons merged with the international firm Touche, to become Touche, Ross.)

P.D. Ross was the first of five sons and three daughters. The other four sons went directly from school into the accountancy firm, but P.D. (as he became known to most of his friends) declined accountancy and took a B.Sc. (engineering, with honours) at McGill. Why he chose engineering was never clear to his family. He had been a hungry reader as a boy and alone of the five brothers was early enchanted by literature. But in a collection of some of his stories he privately printed in 1931, *Retrospects of a Newspaper Person*, he does tell how he got his first newspaper job. As to why he sought it, there is only this line: "I wanted to be a newspaperman."

This was, after all, reason enough, and it certainly proved to be. As often in this memoir of mine, I want to let him tell his own story:

> I graduated from the engineering school of McGill University in 1878, and got a job on the engineering staff of the Montreal Harbor Commission. This lasted well enough for a year or so, but I wanted to be a newspaper man. At McGill, as one of the editors of the McGill College *Gazette*, I had "got the bug."
>
> From a friend was obtained a letter of introduction to Hugh Graham, alias Lord Atholstan, proprietor of the Montreal *Star*, and I presented myself in the Montreal *Star* office, April 25, 1879, to ask for work.
>
> Mr. Graham obviously did not desire to have me wished on him. He said he was afraid he did not have any kind of work to give that would suit me.
>
> "There is no vacancy on our editorial staff," he emphasized. "In any case, it is our policy to take on men only as junior reporters or junior clerks to begin with."
>
> I would like to be a junior reporter.
>
> "Are you doing anything now?" Mr. Graham asked.
>
> "Working on the Harbor Commission—on the engineering staff."
>
> "Ah—may I ask what pay are you getting there?"
>
> "Twenty-five dollars a week."
>
> Mr. Graham's gloom seemed to lift. "That is good pay for a young man," he remarked in a tone which suggested that he thought the trouble was all over. "We don't do anything like that for a start in the newspaper business. We pay inexperienced new reporters $5 a week."
>
> "Thank you very much, Mr. Graham," I said. "When can I come?"
>
> Mr. Graham looked perturbed—but rose to the emergency. "Oh, when you like, I suppose."

Athlete, Then Journalist

Vigor in writing and drive brought him to the post of City Editor within six months. Restlessness took him off in 1882 to become Sports Editor of the Toronto Mail—a likely job, for he was even then a great athlete. In 1883 he became assistant editor of the Toronto *News*, and by 1885 he was back at the Montreal *Star* as Managing Editor: from cub to top job in five years and on Canada's largest paper!

Before journalism had come sports. This six-foot-two, lean-faced, eagle-eyed man shared with his brothers a zest and brilliance in sports of all kinds. He made the McGill football team in his first year, aged 15, and captained it for two years including the game when it played Harvard in the Dominion's first international rugby football match. He organized the McGill hockey team, played right wing. He won the single shells Quebec title, and stroked four-oared crews to many victories. He starred at lacrosse, gymnastics, fencing, boxing, and bulled great strength into a war canoe. Even after really getting into journalism he kept at sports, still winning titles in various of them. In Toronto he stroked a Dominion champion four-oared crew and won the single shell championship of Toronto Bay. In 1886 he stroked a four-oared Lachine boat to a surprise victory over Toronto Argonauts and Ottawa for the Canadian title.

To Ottawa in 1885

Ross was sent to Ottawa as the *Star*'s man in the Parliamentary Press Gallery—a move that led to his interest in *The Ottawa Journal*. The launching of that venture, his buying half of it in 1886 and the other half in 1891, we have from his own hand, again from *Retrospects:*

> Alexander Smith Woodburn started *The Ottawa Evening Journal* Dec. 10, 1885. In the following year I bought a half interest in the paper from him for $4,000, mostly borrowed, becoming joint publisher of *The Journal* on Jan 1, 1887.
>
> No one would have paid 4,000 cents for a half interest in *The Journal* at that time had he known anything about the business side of a newspaper. *The Journal* had been losing money from the start. There were no assets. The plant was merely leased from Mr. Woodburn. The paper was printed on a press belonging to Mr. Woodburn's job printing business. It was printed with Mr. Woodburn's type. It was printed in Mr. Woodburn's establishment. My purchase did not give me any interest in these things. What I bought was merely a half interest in the name and "good-will" of *The Evening Journal*. And so far as

"good-will" was concerned, the willing *Journal* had run behind several thousand dollars in the first year's operation. The circulation of *The Journal* when I joined in was about 1,700, of which 600 were "dead-heads"—namely, free papers to somebody. . . .

Mr. Woodburn had a large job printing business, with which my purchase had no connection. The newspaper was a separate undertaking. He was a first-class printer, an artist in that line. At one time the job printing had been prosperous. At the time we joined forces in *The Journal*, the job printing business was losing ground. His launch into the publication of a newspaper was, for him, a leap in the dark, prompted, no doubt, by the hope that it would help his job printing. The result was the reverse; it made things worse. . . .

To resume the story: Here, in 1887, were Mr. Woodburn and I linked together in the conduct of a losing newspaper business in which both of us were tyros. Followed a hectic time for me. *The Journal* scraped along, losing money, Mr. Woodburn making what advances he could, while I borrowed any more money I could, laboring all the while to learn something of practical business and finance, while also writing editorials and running the news end of the paper. It was tough job. Sometimes on Fridays it was necessary to get out to skirmish for money to pay the wages. Once or twice there was temporary failure to get it, and the staff nearly walked out on us. The struggle began to seem vain, until in 1890 we clearly reached the end of our tether. Money and credit both gone, considerable debt left. I decided to quit. I applied for a job as editor of a weekly paper in the then very remote far northwest, the Fort Macleod *Gazette*, which I heard was vacant. My application was accepted.

Meanwhile I had gone to Mr. Woodburn to offer to sell him my share in *The Journal* cheap. Mr. Woodburn couldn't offer me anything. . . .

Charles Magee, president of the Bank of Ottawa, was president of the Central Fair. As a director I made his acquaintance. It was little more than an acquaintance, for we did not meet often otherwise.

Then, in the summer of 1891, almost on the eve of my packing my trunk for Fort Macleod, a message came to *The Journal* office that Mr. Magee wanted to see me. I went to his private office, an unpretentious place on Elgin street, next to the old *Free Press* building and facing the City Hall. The conversation that ensued has left a vivid impression with me.

Mr. Magee: "Good morning, Mr. Ross. Thank you for coming over. What I want to see you about is this:—The Central Fair will be on soon, and I would like you to take charge of the gates this year."

Myself: "Glad to do it, Mr. Magee, if I were going to be here, but I will be away."

Mr. Magee: "Holiday?"

Myself: "No, leaving Ottawa for good."

Mr. Magee: "Why, how is that?"

Myself: "Well—between ourselves, *The Journal* is up salt creek, I'm out, and I've booked a job elsewhere."

Mr. Magee: "You mean that *The Journal* will stop? Sorry to hear that. I like the paper. Perhaps I could help you."

Myself: "I am afraid not. The trouble is not merely money, though we are losing that, but although I think a great deal of Mr. Woodburn, he and I are not a good newspaper combination. No use our going further together."

Mr. Magee: "Can you buy him out?"

Myself: "Easily enough, if I had any money."

Mr. Magee: "Suppose you find out what he wants—then we could consider further."

I returned disconsolate to Mr. Magee. "Nothing doing," I reported to him. "Mr. Woodburn wants $4,000 and won't budge."

Mr. Magee: "Can you say to me that you have a chance of success with that paper?"

Myself: "I don't know. Maybe."

Mr. Magee: "If you can say so, I'll endorse your note for $4,000."

Myself: "This is rather wonderful, Mr. Magee, and thank you very much, but you don't understand. There is no security. *The Journal* has no assets—nothing but debts. Mr. Woodburn prints it. He owns all the plant. The paper is losing money. I haven't got any money left and couldn't carry on."

Mr. Magee: "If you tell me that you think you have a chance of success, I'll endorse your note for $4,000, and I will help you to form a little company to carry on with."

Myself: "With some capital, there will be a chance."

Mr. Magee: "Go ahead."

The Journal company was duly organized by Mr. Magee, with $30,000 nominal capital. Mr. Magee, G.H. Perley (afterwards Sir George) and N. Charles Sparks, each paid $5,000 cash for stock at par. The other $15,000 stock was allotted to me as paid up, as a consideration for the good-will and the dubious property. It was very generous treatment of me. The cash put in by the others gave *The Journal* a good new start, and after three anxious years we got around the corner.

Reporters Were $6.00 a Week

What was it like putting out a paper in the 1880's? Ross didn't save many documents, but I have one which serves as a springboard to imagination. In his own hand, on a slip of paper 4 x 6 inches, is the "*Journal* Salary and Wage List, Jan. 22, 1887":

General Manager, P.D. Ross	*per week*	$30
Business Department		
Abbott, business manager		12
Bradbury, Advtg solicitor		10
Jeffreys, collector		10
Chamberlain, clerk		7
Kelly (boy)		2
Editorial Staff		
Colquhorn, editor		20
Harkin, city editor		14
McIver, reporter		10
Smith, reporter		6
King, reporter		4
McNeil, proof reader		6
Cronin, (boy)		1
Composing Room		
Thoburn, foreman		14
Flatters, ass't foreman		7
Staff, 16 and $2.50 to $6.00		69
	Total	$222.

Hard by that slip of paper, though, is another which confuses yet clarifies the picture. Also dated Jan. 22, 1887, it adds several to the Composing and Editorial Staffs and the cost of his carriers at a total of $23 per week, bringing the grand total to $283.70. It is written on the back of two long sheets of government stationery. On their front side they were printed tender sheets for suppliers to fill out the provisions and services they undertook to deliver to Indian Agents. The two sheets, pasted together by Mr. Ross, made a ceremonial paper two feet long. In Mr. Ross' always clear hand, across the full width of a sheet of foolscap, is this:

Statement of Journal Business
Jan. 1 to March 31, 1887

RECEIPTS		EXPENDITURES	
Cash	$1,204.50	*Cash*	$3,236.00
Advertising Earned	1,913.34	Due & Accrued	
		March 31 but not paid:	
Subscriptions due first		Paper	700
April from Jan. 1 unpaid	1,000	Rent, gas and	
		Presswork	600
	Total 4,117.84		
		Ross	325
Amount of Advt'd due			
March 31 payable		subtotal $1,625	
in goods	267.80	TOTAL	$4,861.00

Perhaps being alone spurred this sportsman, for under his control the paper was quick off the mark. In the year 1892 Receipts from Advertising were $18,702.72; with Subscriptions of $10,985.27 the total Receipts were $29,687.99. Working expenses were $24,198.81, personal $2,858.51, for a total of $27,057.32—meaning a surplus of $2,630.67. But I like the frankness of Mr. Ross in his penned asterisk-note on the statement: "Note: no allowance made for wear and tear." Observe Statements B of the 1892 report:

Working Expenses, 1892

Wages	$14,412.60
Paper	4,708.60
Telegraphs	998.04
Correspondents	446.45
Commissions	402.32
Postage, etc.	97.70
Rent	800.00
Miscellaneous	963.83
Interest, discount, renewals, etc.	1,369.27
Drawn by P.D. Ross	2,858.51
	$27, 057.32

That's all it took to start one of the great annals in Canadian journalism —plus blood, sweat, tears, guts, and a little bit o' luck! In any case, by 1892 he was on his way. There may have been occasional arrangements for temporary financial assistance but (to make a giant step forward in terms) all signals were now go.

All This, and Marriage, Too!
In 1891 Ross had married Mary Littlejohn, daughter of Col. and Mrs. W.W. Littlejohn of Plymouth, North Carolina—a love and companionship that endured until her death in 1943 and, you might say, warmed him for the remaining six years of his own life. But a look at their early years invites wonder how he got time for home life.

In 1891 he played right wing for the Ottawa Hockey Team: during three of his five years with it, the team won the Ontario Hockey Association championship. In 1892 he became president of the Ottawa Valley McGill Graduates. In 1893 he was appointed one of the first two trustees of the Stanley Cup, by His Excellency Lord Stanley, a task he filled actively until he died. In 1894, he was president of the Ottawa Rowing Club, which had a "wonderful" surplus of $34 that year; he helped it with money and zeal for 55 years. In 1902 he was elected to a two-year term as Alderman. In 1905 he and Mayor Ellis established Ottawa Hydro and thus began his life-long interest in giving cheap power to all Ontario. In 1908 he was named president of the Ottawa Conservative Association. In 1909, he was President of the Royal Canadian Golf Association. In 1912, "I ran for Mayor and was licked by Charles Hopewell, afterwards Ottawa's very excellent Police Magistrate." In 1913 he built and occupied the Journal building, at 237 Queen street.

An Eye On Everything
Yet all the while he was building and running a newspaper in the capital, at a time when the owner-editor had to have an eye on everything. Five old sheets of paper convey "Instructions to the City Editor and Telegraph Editor for 1906." Here are some of the 34 orders, bearing Ross' handwriting:

> The weather must always go on page 10 as it is governed by advertising contract arrangements. The serial story must always go on the same page and until further notice the sporting page will be page 20.
>
> Exercise economy and carefulness in the matter of copy paper, electric light, stationery, etc, etc.
>
> No cut (picture) is to be used a second time without the consent of the managing editor except in the case of the demise of the subject.
>
> Early in the morning bulletins must be put out (on the street) piece by piece. The boy must not be allowed to wait until he has a sheet full.
>
> W.C.T.U. and other temperance matters must be kept off the pages where liquor advertisements are inserted.
>
> Police Court must be inserted daily without fail as it is too important a feature to be lightly left out.
>
> The addresses of houses of ill fame must not be given.
>
> Where a story affects the reputation of anyone, it must not be published without the person concerned having been given a chance to give his version—except where the managing editor otherwise decides.
>
> City Editor and Telegraph Editor will please carry out strictly the long standing rule against copying from *The Citizen*. *The Citizen* must only be used as a source of information as to matter of which we did not know. *The Journal* must be compiled just as though *The Citizen* did not exist.

*   *   *

Even in those now quaint early instructions we can sense the concern Ross was to stress in later years that a newspaper should have a high conscious-ness of responsibility. In this he often expressed his "luck" that he was joined by two men who shared his principles and, as he put it once to a large meeting, "added their own heart and breadth to them": E. Norman Smith and Grattan O'Leary. My father teamed up with Ross in 1917 when his own paper, the *Ottawa Free Press*, amalgamated with *The Journal*, E.N.S. becoming *The Journal*'s editor and vice-president. Grattan O'Leary, that gifted and wonderful latter-day sprite, had come to *The Journal* in 1911 as a reporter and succeeded my father as editor and president in 1957.

But let's not rush ahead from those earlier days of adventure. When *The Journal* celebrated its fortieth birthday on Dec. 12, 1925, Ross received a great collection of messages and I have those letters. One I suspect moved him more than the tributes from prominent people. It was from Ellie Cronin Connell, of 522 Gladstone avenue, Ottawa. She had worked for *The Journal* from Dec. 11, 1886 until the time of her marriage in November of 1896, and recalled those bygone days:

My retrospect visualizes the ramshackle building on Elgin street where in the springtime mornings at 7 o'clock and through the ensuing hours we hopped the puddles on the floor which had dripped through the ice-and-snow-soaked roof. Inverted type boxes and wood blocks served as stepping stones, but we rose above the situation with *Comin' Through the Rye*, because we were young. During a period of financial embarassment such as might happen anywhere since money is the substance, ghost and re-incarnation of all enterprise, the other women members of the staff and myself *stuck* by Mr. Thoburn and Mr. Flatters while the male members *struck*. With active minds and nimble fingers we set the minion and long primer type and had the really thrilling satisfaction of seeing and hearing the forms closed and the press rattling on schedule time for you, while the men stood with their backs to the wall of Devlin's old fur shop where ox-robes waved like cable banners in the breeze. We realized that we were competent and this made us confident. We were young. Some of the girls have passed into the Beyond, or that mysterious place where the Creator makes his matrices, but three of them survive and we often talk of our *Journal* days. Not one of our quartette left *The Journal* for financial betterment; marriage was the reason.

And In Came Grattan!

It was only 15 years after those days Ellie Cronin Connell describes that Grattan O'Leary came along—in 1911. In May, 1973, I told Grattan of the book I was planning and asked if I might bring my tape-recorder along to his room in the Senate, to get him talking of old times. He was then only 86, and had almost instant total recall!

A very ramshackle set-up was the *Journal* office in the old building on Elgin street, Grattan remembered. Ross had an office to himself in the corner but didn't come into the news room much and Grattan scarcely laid eyes on him in the first year. Only after that did he really meet him—though Grattan had been writing the parliamentary news. Grattan relates the meeting this way:

> One day he had an editorial on the American constitution which I thought was silly. So, foolishly, I sat down and wrote a letter to the editor in which I denounced this editorial as unhistorical and superficial. I quoted what Cardinal Newman had said about the American constitution and quoted Macaulay as having said the constitution was all sail and no anchor, and so on. I sent the letter into the office and next day Jim Muir the Managing Editor said "P.D. Ross would like to talk to you." I thought this was the end. So I went and knocked on his door and got admitted and he had the letter in front of him. He said "O'Leary, did you write that letter?" "Yes sir." "Well, I just called you in to tell you that any time you want to start writing editorials for the paper I'll be glad to have them." That's all he said.

O'Leary did start writing editorials, and soon it was his main job. He was amazed at the rein Ross gave him from the beginning. Once when Ross was going away on a holiday Grattan knew a case was coming before the Privy Council regarding separate schools, a touchier subject then than now. Before Ross left, Grattan asked for advice on how to handle it. Ross, let's remember, was a Protestant and Grattan a Catholic. "He looked at me in a somewhat stern way and said: 'O'Leary, you say what you think is sensible,' and that was it."

As time went on, it seems Ross and he did little conferring about things. It was a form of tribute to Grattan, but the Irishman who was more accustomed to defending his freedom seemed almost to find it embarrassing:

> He didn't even look at my editorials. He never came in in the evening. One day before going to play golf he wrote an editorial and sent it upstairs himself; I wrote one on the same subject and sent mine up. Both appeared next day, absolutely contradictory! That was P.D.!
>
> He used to go off on tangents. On the Irish question, for instance. After one of his editorials I wrote a letter, oh a vicious letter, and he published it. Next day he wrote a scarifying piece on me and said where I should be was down in Tammany Hall in New York. I went in and said. "Well Mr. Ross, I guess this means I'm fired." He said, "Don't be silly."
>
> He was quite a powerful writer when he was moved by something, but to say he was a good editor is not true. Mr. Ross took absolutely no interest in External Affairs; it would be hard to find an editorial dealing with foreign affairs. But mind you we must look at this in the context in which we lived here. My God, I mean the Royal Standard floated over the East Block and the Governor General came to his office there every day. This was an English colony, no question about this.
>
> P.D. never ran for Parliament, he was more interested in civic than federal politics. As an alderman for several years, and in all the posts he was asked to fill when not an alderman, he worked hard at civic problems. He'd be in the office studying the returns on civic election night but I never saw him in the office on federal election night.

Well, whoa a minute, Grattan, I wanted to say—but when you have him in flight before a tape-recorder you just don't want to break the spell. But there again, his seeming to criticise Ross for relatively little interest in federal politics and for not going into the shop on general election nights may, through modesty, completely miss the point. Ross knew Grattan knew his stuff in federal politics, and as an athlete and coach he knew also it wouldn't do Grattan any harm if he fell on his face some time in a major editorial at a crucial time. He knew his man, sensed his future and—why go down to fuss around when the returns are coming in? To spell it still further—if Ross had gone down, he'd have to take a hand—and in that case Grattan might well have wished to Heaven he'd go home!

The Merger
I asked whether the merger in 1917 of the Conservative *Journal* and the Liberal *Free Press* caused much interest or concern. Grattan replied as follows:

I don't think the average man cared. You see, P.D. was a Conservative when the election drums rolled, but between elections he wasn't really. He was a pretty independent-minded man, and your father was, too. There was really never any real problem, though in one election there was a Conservative meeting in Eastview and I was the guest speaker and P.D. Ross came out and took the Chair! Bloody nonsense for the paper really, crazy; I would have advised against it if I had known it was going to happen. Specially as there wasn't a possibility of winning the damn election! Your Dad didn't like that. He mentioned it to me. He said "This is no good for you, no good for Mr. Ross, and no good for the paper." And he was right.

As to the amalgamation, concern was felt by the employees of each paper, which ones would lose their jobs. Your Dad insisted on the continued employment of many of his key people. Tommy Lowrey came over as City Editor. Ross Munro, father of your friend the great war correspondent and Southam publisher, came over and became *The Journal*'s Managing Editor! Munro also used to write a column, "From the Sixth Floor"—we thought that was very high up. We had a morning and evening paper then, the Morning continued until July 2, 1949.

O'Leary was not very "high" on the method of operation of the old *Journal*, but perhaps that becomes understandable when we note that Grattan says "On pay day they used to go over and negotiate the payment with the bank, they didn't have the money." He continues:

26

If you go back to *The Journal* of 1911, 1912, 1913—it was a complete mess. It wasn't a newspaper at all. The fact that he would go away for two or three months in the winter to play golf and leave the editorials to a youngster like me was unbelievable. You see, P.D. had no ideology about anything, he was a contradiction, completely, politically. As a Free Trader he supported reciprocity in a column-long editorial and three weeks later turned absolutely against reciprocity. He was mad against public ownership and all in favor of private enterprise, yet Hydro was a God for him and Sir Adam Beck was his great hero, who was the father of hydro electric in Ontario—public ownership. You never could quite place P.D., just where he stood on questions.

You see—compare your Dad with P.D. Now I thought P.D. was a better writer, but your father was a superb editor. The paper only began to become a newspaper after your Dad came over to it. Your Dad took an active interest in everything. But up to that time the paper was —well, it just came out. I often wonder how the paper survived, upon my soul, looking back on it now, from the way it was gotten out.

But Mr. Ross could laugh at himself. Your father had a hell of a fine editorial on him one day. P.D. wrote a tremendous article on reciprocity—some of the things he wrote on reciprocity were unbelievable—and ended it with that old quote "To your Tents, O Israel." The next day your father wrote an editorial in the Free Press saying "The editor of *The Journal*, having summoned Israel to its tents, took the afternoon off and played golf." P.D. thought it was damn good.

Well, again that's Grattan all right—talking of P.D.'s foibles and strengths in successive breaths. He had a great love of the man, really. If anyone else criticised P.D., Grattan would tear the skin off him.

Ross may not have been much on routine, but in his courage, his judgment of principles and men, he stood against all the tests.

The Ross Family
Before moving further along in years, I think we should sense something of the family atmosphere in which Ross grew up. It wasn't pioneer Canada, but it wasn't just yesterday, either. His nephew, Howard Ross, who became

head of P.S. Ross and Sons, then Chancellor of McGill and then dean of its Faculty of Business Management, helped me immensely in this.

It appears that Philip S. Ross, the grandfather, drove himself very hard to get ahead—the Bible and his account books always close by. The five boys had always his full support in their changing careers, though he had often to dig them out with cash from his scant reserves. As young men they dabbled in real estate, in buying prairie farmsites, in oil, and in gambling on property in the Thousand Islands. P.D. did less of this for he knew where he was going (and that too was gamble!). All but P.D. became chartered accountants, and only the third son William left the father's firm. He became president of the Asbestos Corporation of Quebec, ran the Windsor Hotel, became President of Montreal Tramways, and Chairman of the Montreal Harbours Commission. For years P.D. had his brother Jim (Major General James G. Ross in World War 1) on the Board of *The Journal* as a financial expert. Howard tells a yarn about that:

> When Uncle Jim was about 85 and not very well, he suggested to P.D. that he ought to get a younger man on the board. P.D. said that was a great idea and suggested they get John, my Father, who was only 76. So they went to him and said they wanted a younger man on the Board. Dad said "Don't be crazy, why don't you take Howard?" I suppose I happened to be in the outer office at the moment. That's how I became a Director of *The Journal*.

And a lucky thing for us he did, showing us the mysteries of finance and management and the under-tows ready to catch us if we didn't watch out.

To go back a bit: Grandfather Ross had written with great frequency to P.D. of the goings-on at the accounting office and throughout the family, in Canada and back home. He was a strong family man, right proud of P.D. and at pains to say so all the way. But he would balance stirring Biblical injunctions with Scottish canniness, urging P.D. not to be so kind to others as to be foolish. Of the brothers only P.D. was interested in politics: the others were closer to the view often asserted by Grandfather, "Thank God I was never minded to get mixed up in politics and that dirty business." P.D. urged every young man to get interested in politics, it didn't matter which party. There seemed a special link between P.D. and his mother, perhaps because he was away from home. She it was who gave him the $4,000 to buy his half-share in *The Journal*. "That was probably her whole life dowry and savings. She kept backing him to the hilt in affection," Howard says, "and it was a love Uncle Phil returned and never forgot, he taking care to look after her relatives in his will fifty years later. She was to all of us a very lovely, outgoing, attractive person. I knew her, for she lived four years longer than my Grandfather, dying in 1911."

There's an early story of P.D.'s father and mother Howard says was passed on by Sam Campbell, the oldest grandson:

> It seems that in the middle of a family picnic with the whole clan Grandfather collapsed. They got him home and laid him out on the sofa and sent a youngster over to the family doctor, Alexander Blackader. The boy came back and said the doctor was at dinner but would come over after. Grandma said. "You go right back there, son, and tell Dr. Blackader to come immediately. This is important." So Dr. Blackader came over, carrying his serviette to show he had been disturbed at dinner, in a very bad temper. He took one look at Grandfather and said, "He'll be all right, he's simply dead drunk, and stamped out. Grandmother never spoke to Dr. Blackader again, Sam said. I think there's probably something in that story.

But Howard thinks none of the five sons was much impressed with liquor. "P.D. and Uncle Jim and Dad were not teetotallers, and kept a decanter of Scotch around to prove they weren't, but they hardly drank. Once they gave a bang-up dinner for Uncle Jim when he won a snowshoe race or something; I've got the menu around and it says, 'The dinner will be conducted on temperance principles.' I think Uncle Willie and Uncle Al may have drunk a bit more, they were poker players and more convivial types."

Howard sensed Mr. Ross had been rather a lonely man, and that apart from his wife, to whom he was completely devoted, he had very few close friends. "If you spend most of your time working and reading, do you get time to make friends? I think I remember his mentioning only two men as close to him—Sir George Perley and his doctor Campbell Laidlaw, and perhaps Sir Robert Borden. Not having children may have added to Uncle Phil's loneliness, although I'm not sure. He had a raft of nephews and nieces but I think my sister Phyllis was the only one Uncle Phil and Aunt Mary felt deep affection for—perhaps initially because she had not been well and they had the joy of aiding her recovery.''

My own guess is that P.D.'s interest in sport reduced the number of *close* personal friends. His being interested and active in nearly every sport, and they changing each season, the scores of friends old and new in them kept him ''occupied'' and ''unlonely''. Even with his brothers—their letters relate mainly to sports. They were all good athletes. Jim and Willie won every kind of championship: snowshoeing, paddling, track. ''Uncle Jim once wrote P.D. on how to train, and his ideas were pretty spartan. He then gave his times—he was a distance man rather than a sprinter—at half-mile, mile, three miles, on snowshoes and on track, and ended up by saying 'As you will see, I am within a fraction of the world's record time on each one of these distances.' ''

Were the Ross brothers professional Scots? ''Not in a sort of offensive way. They weren't members of the St. Andrew's Society, or anything like that. They were terribly proud of being Scottish, and of how their father had got ahead and made a place for them in this new land. But they didn't wear the kilt or anything like that.''

Finally, what place had religion in the Ross family?

''Certainly Grandfather and Grandmother must have been quite narrow Scottish Presbyterian, and the boys were all brought up that way. My father and his twin brother Alex, and Uncle Jim, were all church elders, deeply involved in the fight for church union. In our family we used to go to church every Sunday without fail, and as kids we went to Sunday school in the afternoon. We also held a song service in our country house in the evening. I can remember, for instance, when Dad first allowed tennis to be played on Sunday. He used to insist that whatever we read during the week, we'd have to read Pilgrim's Progress or something or other on Sunday. Though we played a lot of cards, I suppose Dad got to be 60 before he played his first bridge game on Sunday. I imagine P.D. was pretty much like that, though perhaps not quite so strict.

''Uncle Phil's wife was from Toronto, an Anglican, and he of course was a Presbyterian. When they moved to Ottawa they decided they would go to the Presbyterian church, but the first Sunday they heard a god-awful sermon.

As they came out, Uncle Phil said, 'Well, let's try your man next time.' So they went to All Saints Anglican church on Chapel street and I gather he became a regular attendant—and considerable donor—though I don't believe he ever joined it.

"That led to an incident at P.D.'s funeral which in these days of ecumenical services seems pretty odd. I was arranging the funeral. The rector in charge, a hell of a nice fellow, came to me and said it was very very sad, for the Prime Minister and others were coming and though the Bishop wanted to come he felt that if he came he should take part in the service, perhaps read the Lesson or something, 'but this is going to be very difficult because your Uncle never joined the Church.' Well, I said that was up to the Bishop, of course; and if he felt he could not come that would not create any awkwardness with anybody. However, he returned later and said it had all been fixed up; 'He's going to sit there, but he won't read the Lesson.' I said 'That's fine, it's a splendid arrangement'; so we got through it."

Grattan O'Leary spoke of Ross' almost naive sensitivity about poetry that bordered on the spiritual. "He was a militant Christian in his way, but I don't suppose he ever read a word of theology in his life; he was not concerned with that kind of stuff. He attacked the Jesuit Estates' amassing and holding of wealth and was looked upon in Ottawa as a sort of militant Protestant. Yet whenever nuns or priests or ardent Catholic laymen came to him in some good cause for their church, he was a generous giver. I don't think he had any religious bigotry or prejudice, but on the other hand I can't conceive of his having ever been very very devout."

Well, perhaps not, and yet. . . .

On the occasion of *The Journal's* fiftieth anniversary, Ross wrote an editorial observing that in many material ways Ottawa and the world had moved fast and far in fifty years:

> But this remains the same old world as regards the human spirit, the relations of home and family, of lover and sweetheart, of man and wife, father and son, mother and daughter; of employer and employee, of rich man and poor man, of teacher and pupil, of pulpit and flock. In these relations there is the same old need, the same overwhelming need, of love and faith, of honesty and generosity, of unselfishness and

friendliness, of clean conduct and fair play. And the truth remains still much as it stood fifty years ago, that these last mentioned things are more important to humanity than all the achievements of art and science and mechanical invention from the beginning of the world, or all that can be, until the end of it.

He Faces the Questions of His Time: Labor

Let's have a look now at the man as he was in his prime, in relation to the big questions of the day. The financial problems of his paper were rough, but in a Labor magazine published in Ottawa at the turn of the century he wrote these thoughts about the Eight Hour Day—fifty years before it was generally accepted:

> . . . Work an average man twelve hours a day, and you get the horse-end and only that, and you ensure that nothing more will ever be got from him, and probably little more from his sons. An ounce of brain is worth a ton of muscle.
>
> The duty of employers and of the public ceases when labor reaches a point at which a good living can be earned by the average workman yet leave him spare energy and vitality for something besides his bread-winning. An eight-hour day is not far from that point.
>
> But don't expect a miracle. A man who gets an eight-hour day won't go home after his work and start to learn the Encyclopaedia Britannica by heart. Thank God, there will be something better for him to do than that—leisure to look about him, time to do more for and with his wife and children, freedom to respect himself as something better than a beast of burden, opportunity to take an intelligent interest of some kind or another in the doings of the community about him.
>
> In this and many other respects, humanity may thank heaven for the results of the labor unions. The injustice they have done is milk and water to the injustice they have banished. Certainly they have been narrow at times, bigoted, wrong, violent and cruel. But where were the unions born? They were born among men who were driven like brutes and slaves. As the conditions of labor have ameliorated, as the brains and bodies of workingmen have both got better food, the unions have gained moderation and fairness.

Human Welfare

In 1909 a trip to England and Scotland broadened his horizons. Though it was to attend a meeting of the Imperial Press Union, he moved around the country a good deal and made a special effort to see not just the monuments and the important people but the working people and farmers and how they lived. His address on returning home, to the Empire Club in Toronto, was a mixture of awe and concern. He had left Britain "more warmly British at heart" than when he arrived. The various forms of class institutions and class education disappointed him, and Canada should not want to become "too closely identified" with that kind of system. However, he did acquire more than ever a desire "to remain leagued with her courage and energy and honesty; with her independence and self-reliance; with her great history, her great literature, her great and sane freedom." They had left England feeling a new pride in British fame, "a new determination to help it out, if we could, and a new hope and a new confidence in an enduring British Empire of world-wide partnership."

Now that is stirring stuff, and perhaps expectable from one of his stock and in a talk to the Empire Club. Yet Ross occasionally used to strike out at the old British lion and sometimes perhaps with a touch more of anger than perspective. I recall one editorial he wanted to write (and did) in the second great war which roundly berated Britain's conduct of the war, and that produced fiery argument in memo form from none other than the Irishman Grattan O'Leary! Ross still wanted to run it, and Grattan to run his substitute; but my father; the Englishman 'twixt Scot and Irish, found some middle way which was doubtless better sense but a duller editorial!

But that is an aside. I want to return to Ross' trip to England and what may have been a more significant reaction to it—an awakening or sharpening of his social conscience. "Take me," he said to a guide in London, "through the worst parts of London. Go all afternoon, go to the dirtiest slums, to the poorest and to the worst people." And he did the same in Manchester, Glasgow and Sheffield. It appalled him—"masses of dwarfed, half-starved, wretched-looking people." From then on the editorial page of *The Journal* took on a more zealous concern in improving the lot of the Canadian workingman and frequently crusaded for new social policies that were the more effective for coming from a nominally Conservative editor and paper.

His genuine concern in human welfare involved Ross in a variety of enquiries and organizations in that field. It doubtless led to his being named head of the Royal Commission established in 1930 by the Ontario Government to review the province's organization of social welfare. After the report came down he addressed the Canadian Life Insurance Officers Association. It must have given them a bit of a shock to hear the Chief Commissioner begin by saying theirs was "in one respect at least a defective report," for he noted the main reaction was, "Where would the money come from?" The need for reform had been told in statistics through its 110 pages, he said, "but they were disjointed and you miss the cumulative force." The recommended added expenditure of $2,500,000 a year, much less than a dollar a head for every Ontario citizen, would improve conditions in every type of hospital sanatorium, asylum, reformatory, jail, and children's aid centre. It would aid the crippled and blind, orphans and aged; it would train nurses and special service agents.

The Commissioners, he said, were awed by two chief impressions:

(1) The tremendous waste we saw of human life and human energies—scores of thousands of human beings, miserable or useless or worse in this comparatively small province.

(2) The faces of the children, 30,000 of them. These young souls looking out of questioning eyes are facing the future of life with no fair chance of happiness, with little love, with little hope!

Imagine, at the close of this meeting of insurance heads, that rangy athlete quoting Elizabeth Barrett Browning:

"Yes, we are weary" say the children
"We can not run or climb,
"It is good when it happens," say the children.
"That we die before our time."

Education
That insight into his feeling for the young leads me to a talk he prepared for the boys of Ashbury College, in Ottawa, in 1937, and an address on the meaning of a university, which he gave to McGill in 1935 on his being made a Doctor of Laws, *honoris causa*.

To Ashbury he put the proposition that a boy should be a "a generous chap who goes in for fair play for everybody and everything, and perhaps a little more than fair play, a fellow who is clean and straight with himself and with all others."

Strange, but almost I can hear those words coming from him, not as the clichés they may read like—but direct, clear, like a punch on the nose. And these:

> Being square with oneself means a fellow must live clean with his stomach, clean with his mind. A fellow doesn't have to try to be a saint altogether, but if you want to be the real thing, in business or athletics, you've got to live good and clean.
>
> Being square with other people means that you would want to do the decent thing not only with your friends but even with those who do not happen to be exactly your friends. Above all, it would mean trying to be to your father and mother as good a son as you can be, in short, to love them, to love them good and hard. The home is the most important place in the world for any of us.

To McGill University Ross made what he called a brief confession of faith in universities:

> If in youth we chance to ascend a mountain-top our eyes range over a wide expanse of hills and valleys, green fields and hamlets, homes and industries. Our eyesight is no better, our brain is no better, but our outlook is vastly different. And if we have to fare forth in this new world we will do so with a pleasure and confidence which could hardly have been ours had we known only what came within our ken on the lower level. Such should be the mental effect of university education. The university offers to our minds a panoramic survey of all that lies behind us in human history, and a better view of all that lies around us in human achievement. It helps us to a better imagination of the future and opens the wide range of history and life in understandable proportions.

I Started By Lying to Him!
May I now set down my own recollections? My first "encounter" with Mr.

Ross was when, about ten years old, I had come in with Dad from the cottage at Aylmer on the suburban street car about eight in the morning. He put me then on the Bank Street car to the Exhibition and went to the office. About 3:45, broke and weary and sick from pink floss, I came to the office to wait for Dad to go home. My friend Alf Trafford the elevator man used to let me run the up-and-down lever, keeping a close eye on me; on bringing the craft to a jerky halt at the main floor who stepped out but Mr. Ross! He knew me all right, but said sternly: "What are you doing here?" I mumbled in falsehood and confusion that I was going to the Exhibition. "Well, you better go then," he said. Alf and Mr. Ross and I rode up the six floors in silence. He took one step out, paused, reached into his pocket and gave me 25 cents and told me I'd get better rides out at the Midway. His eyes twinkled a bit at Alf as he went off, I'm sure. As a quarter in those days was indecent wealth I didn't want to give up, because I knew I had lied, and because I had been caught running the machine, I asked Alf not to tell Dad. I suppose he did, but Dad kept his secret!

From 1928 when I started with *The Journal* until the early 1940's when I got into parliamentary and editorial page work I saw very little of Mr. Ross. He would occasionally stride into the news room, quickly turn up an item in a back paper, jot down a note or two and stride out. If someone were in his path he would politely say good morning, but otherwise no mixing—unless Tom Lowrey the managing editor, or Baz O'Meara or Walter Gilhooly or Bill Westwick the sports editors were handy, and then they'd chat of sport with easy friendship and loud guffaws. As O'Leary and Lowrey have recalled, he was not greatly interested in the getting out of the paper—he had done enough of that and the hard way. I don't recall hearing of his taking a hand in planning news coverage, handling staff or promotions or salaries, nor many occasions when he spoke or wrote in criticism or congratulation to the staff.

But I never heard of a staffer feeling, let alone saying, that P.D. was an autocrat or a poor publisher. The staff held him in awe, with a touch of fear in it, and great respect. He, with my father and Grattan and Tom Lowrey put out a respectable paper and ran a happy shop. So to the builder went ungrudging though distant admiration. In turn, he was repeatedly warm in praise of his senior associates, publicly and in the building: "While I hate to say it to their faces I don't think anyone ever had a more splendid lot of business associates. They run the paper—they are the real doctors now —although they do their best not to let me know it.''

I remember well the first talk I had with him when, aged 29, I rejoined *The Journal* in 1938 after being with The Canadian Press for eight years in various Canadian cities and New York and London. I suppose that absence had deepened my awe of him when he invited me into his office and plied me with questions about what I had been doing. The questions grew pretty specific, what was the CP cross-Canada structure now, what had it been like covering the Saskatchewan elections, what was the cost of overseas cables, had I written much sports, was Reuters any good—and, oh yes, which did I think was the best paper in England? I said the Manchester Guardian was, and he exploded ''Why, for Pete's sake?'' adding something about it being blind Liberal. I said I thought it was the best written and best edited. ''Well, all right,'' he laughed, ''I guess that's true.'' It seemed to me a good place to quit, and he rose and said, sort of loud and embarrassed, ''Good. We're all glad to have you back. We're all too old around here. Move in easily at first, get the feel of the place, great people around here. Good luck!'' At the door he shook my hand and said: ''One thing more, Norman, don't leave us again.'' A sentence like that one remembers well.

''Unique, effective and old-fashioned''
I moved into the editorial page wing a year and a bit later as a junior. Its narrow corridor and four offices were used by E.N.S., O'Leary, Vernon Kipp and myself. Ross was in the large office in the Northwest corner with the old fashioned leaded windows, square beam ceiling, a gas-log fire which didn't work. A large fern graced the far corner, watered by his devoted secretary Irene Sadler, but the room was innocent of ''show'' other than a few sporting pictures, a filing cabinet which he alone opened, and a great brass spittoon. The desk was plain oak, large and flat; but no typewriter, for he and E.N.S. used only their clear-flowing ''hand.''

I was in P.D.'s office very rarely, and always briefly. O'Leary and Kipp weren't in it much, either. One framed the question one had to make before going in. After knocking lightly and hearing the inevitably pleasant ''good morning'' (he was almost never there in the afternoon) one walked in and, standing, put the point: ''Yes, fine,'' was a likely answer, in full. But so was ''No, I don't like that.'' Occasionally he'd chat to the point of replying with the single word "Why?", but as C.D. Howe said to the Commons, he never wanted to let the matter deteriorate into a debate.

Similarly, he didn't discuss with us what he was going to write. He didn't write often, but when something riled him he'd do two columns. One time he had been at his desk all morning and afternoon and the following morning, writing away, saying nothing to anyone. The second afternoon he dropped on my desk a pile of 63 pages of copy paper 8 by 8 inches square, each bearing about seven lines of handwriting. "Do whatever you want with that, if you think it's all right," he said, and with a sheepish sort of smile he disappeared. I thought it was "all right" and put it into the paper!

The lack of discussion between Ross and the rest of us may sound curious in these days of group decisions and participation. But basically they, and later I, were all fundamentally agreed as to the paper's role and P.D. left it to us to interpret that role to the issues of the day, with what facts we could find, with common sense and good manners. Between E.N.S. and O'Leary and Kipp and myself there was lots of easy discussion, though not in regular "meetings". Presumably P.D. and E.N.S. used to thrash out a point of difference occasionally, but the discussion never got back to us. E.N.S. was not the kind of man to boast he had changed P.D.'s mind, nor would Ross gloat; and Grattan's regard for both was such that he would never have asked. So there it was: unique, effective, and "old-fashioned."

What a break to work under such a threesome, and add the name of Tom Lowrey. Each was his own man, each strong-minded, each with a distinct and distinguished personality. They could laugh or argue and enjoy both. If a situation needed clearing up, they would write each other a very frank memo and the thing would be resolved that day—no grudge, no sulks. I remember my repeated fascination in how when one of them was speaking the others would *listen*, attentively and not preoccupied in framing their replies. None ever spoke or acted as though he was the whole cheese in the office, whether in or outside the building. And Ross specially used almost to boast that he left it all to E.N.S. and Grattan. He used to like telling of William Findlay who had come over to *The Journal* from the *Free Press* in 1917 as Acting General Manager. Findlay said to Ross: "I like the way you run your paper, you never interfere with anybody!" P.D. would roar each time he'd tell it, and the dig in it didn't escape him.

Sir John A.—and Others

Clearly I have a conflict of interests in shaping this story of P.D. Ross —alternating between the man and the journalist. We'll come back to *The Journal*, but here is the immediate itinerary. First, a couple of his tales about Sir John A. Macdonald and others; next, his position on several political issues including Quebec and a dignified disagreement with Arthur Meighen; next a punch on the nose for Mitch Hepburn and a disapproving assessment of Mackenzie King Liberals; and then a simply-worded defence of capitalism as against socialism.

Ross was not one of those boring old men who roam clubs and homes to recall the great old days. He had a good touch as raconteur, cigar in hand and a strong twinkle in his eyes, and he had much to recount. He once said he regarded our first Prime Minister as our greatest statesman and Sir Robert Borden as our noblest character. He knew all of the Prime Ministers from the start of Confederation until his death in 1949. To a group of curling friends in Montreal, headed by his great rink and golfing friend Willie Hodgson, Ross once recalled his first meeting with Sir John Macdonald:

At the time of the Dominion General election of 1882, fifty years ago, you will note, I was a reporter on the staff of the Toronto *Daily Mail*. The *Mail*, which then as now, was the chief Conservative organ, sent me to Kingston to report the proceedings at a big mass meeting to be addressed by the Conservative leader and prime minister, Sir John Macdonald. The meeting was preceded by a grand banquet. At the banquet the liquid refreshments were admirable. Having my duty to do, I conducted myself with proper restraint. This was not the case with many others, including, I am sorry to say, Sir John Macdonald himself. In fact, when the mass meeting convened after the banquet, Sir John was in no condition to make a good speech,—indeed he was just about able to stand up. He realised the situation though, and after some rambling remarks pleaded illness and left the platform, retiring to the hotel he was staying at. There were other prominent speakers for the occasion, so the meeting went on, and I stayed there a couple of hours reporting the proceedings. Then I returned to the hotel to finish my report—the same hotel as Sir John was staying at. When I got there I found a message that Sir John wanted to see the *Mail* reporter. Going up to his room I found him sitting up in bed with a wet towel tied round his head, perfectly sober. This was my first meeting with Sir John.

"What are you doing about my speech?" he enquired.

"Well, I haven't got a very good report, sir," I replied.

"No?" he said, "Well, sit down and I'll give you something."

I got my note book out and Sir John proceeded to make a compact and admirable little speech for fifteen or twenty minutes.

"How will that do?" he asked when he finished.

"Very fine, sir," I said. "Thank you very much."

"All right," he said, "send it off. Good night."

I rose and started to leave the room. Just as I got to the door Sir John called out—"Hold on, wait a minute young man, I want to give you a piece of advice." Fixing me with a glittering eye, and pointing his finger at me, he said, "Never again, young man, attempt to report a public speaker when you are under the influence of liquor."

Notwithstanding my condition on this occasion, Sir John and I remained friends nearly always afterwards, although once indeed he threatened to put me in jail.

Another John A. story he liked was of when Sir Charles Tupper, Maritime Cabinet Minister, sent a man to him who wanted a job. Finding the man was from the Maritimes, Sir John sent him back to Sir Charles. Sir Charles sent him back to Sir John again with a note saying he was a very deserving man. Sir John scribbled something on the note, enclosed it in an envelope and told the man to take it back to Sir Charles and it would be all right. When Sir Charles opened the envelope he found that Sir John had scribbled on the note: "Dear Charlie—Please skin your own skunks."

A memory of Sir John in quite different vein Ross placed in his book, *Retrospects of a Newspaper Person:*

One afternoon in the autumn previous to his death June 6, 1891, which came from paralysis after a stroke, a message came to the *Journal* office that Sir John wanted to see me at his house, Earnscliffe. I proceeded to Earnscliffe. The hour was about half past two. I was shown into the library. Sir John was there alone.

The old man was seated at a little table, by a window, with a pack of cards spread out before him. He looked up.

"How d'ye do, Ross," he said. "Seem to be surprised, I notice."

"I did not suppose you ever looked at a card, sir."

"Ross," he rejoined, "you are getting a side-light upon the beauty of public life. Sometimes I take a half hour to myself after lunch. When Parliament is in session we usually have a cabinet meeting after lunch, as you know, before the House opens at three; and at such times such a debauch as you are witnessing is out of the question. When Parliament is not in session I have precious little spare time anyway. But when I can, I indulge myself after lunch for half an hour with a game of solitaire, or as some people call it, Patience."

He paused a moment, then proceeded: "Outside of my family, where I have always been happy, you see me at the only sort of recreation I have allowed myself during the past thirty years. But I shall reach rest soon."

That personal glimpse of Sir John A. Macdonald leads to one on Sir John Thompson, who succeeded Macdonald as Prime Minister. The story is preceded by Ross talking of the burden carried by our public men:

In the Dominion Archives in Ottawa, there are five hundred volumes—five hundred—of the official correspondence of Sir John A. Macdonald. A great deal of that is in his own handwriting. When you add to this the great pressure of attendance in Parliament, cabinet, meetings with his staff and civil service leaders, and with other public men, you get some idea of the pressure our leaders work under.

I was walking up Elgin Street once with Sir John Thompson, and spoke of a book I had been reading. Sir John seemed interested, "Would you like to see the book?" I asked. "No," said Thompson, "No—no use—I have no time for reading. I am just wearing a rut between my bedroom and my office." He died shortly afterward—on a state visit to England—in Windsor Castle.

Sir Robert Borden

Howard Ross has said he believed Sir Robert Borden was one of Ross' few close friends. That adds poignancy to his tribute to Sir Robert. It was in an "I Remember" series of broadcasts over the National Broadcasting Corporation in 1937, just after Sir Robert's death.

> I cannot mention Sir Robert Borden's name without deep feeling. Sir Robert Borden was not eloquent, although a powerful debater. He was not magnetic. He was a reserved man usually, almost a shy man. His strength was character. . . . He was Honorary President of the Canadian Senior Golfers' Association and accompanied me to one of our annual meets, which that year was at Mount Bruno, near Montreal. We were quartered in a bungalow near the Club House, where my room was opposite Sir Robert's. One morning about six o'clock I was awakened by sound of a loud slapping in a queer jerky way, reverberating through the bungalow. "What the devil is that?" I thought. Then I realised the sounds came from Sir Robert's room. "Hey, good morning!" I called out, in what possibly was a sharp tone. "Hello, good morning P.D." came back in Sir Robert's voice. "Hope I haven't disturbed you. I'm going through my morning exercises. I slap the flesh to promote circulation. I do it to music." Came a lot of zig-zag slaps. Then Sir Robert's voice again: "Do you recognise the rhythm? It's the Toreador song from *Carmen*." And that was that.

In Praise of French Canadians

I never heard P.D. Ross say a single word critical of the French-speaking Canadians, even in the privacy of office or home. His integrity moved him to criticise all Canadians from time to time as he deemed necessary, but he would allow no prejudice against French Canadians as a people, in *The Journal* or in his conversations. I was comforted by that precedent when in my own time as editor though the French issue flamed high into separatism and lawlessness, I felt and wrote a viewpoint that enraged many English readers. Some of the hardest criticism to bear was from readers who said P.D. Ross would never have taken such a stand—but I didn't bring the following article to my defence, for it seemed to me each editor must stand on his own feet. But see how splendidly Ross put it amid the heat of the Riel debate in 1885, in his article *"Fair Play For French Canadians:"*

There is a disposition on the part of many Ontario papers, probably indicative of the feeling of many Ontario people, to believe that the French Canadian element in the Dominion is unwarrantably aggressive in national politics. This feeling appears to have been brought to a head by the rising in the North-West, and to be reaching boiling point over Louis David Riel. Allow me, a Canadian born and bred, as a journalist fairly acquainted with both Ontario and Quebec, an English-speaking Protestant, and, I believe, a fair-minded man, to state my conviction that a considerable proportion of the press and people of Ontario are every whit as narrow-minded in matters of race and creed as our French-speaking countrymen can be, as aggressive and every whit as blamable for any friction which exists between the two peoples.

A Toronto paper a few days ago published the following editorial paragraph: "Hang Riel with the French flag—it is all that rag is good for." The French flag is nothing to Canadians, either French or English-speaking, save as representing an idea; and what was implied was that anything likely to be deeply respected by French-speaking Canadians was good enough only to hang a murderer with.

I do not think that English fair play has been shown in the slightest degree by many Ontario people to French-speaking Canadians in the matter of the half-breed rising. The disposition of French-speaking Canadians to make allowances for Riel has been exaggerated. The idiocy of a few law students, the screams of Les Métis, have been grabbed at as representative of a race. I do not think I go too far when I say that the great majority of French-speaking Canadians have never condoned Riel's part in the rebellion further than to insist that, for the sake of justice to the half-breeds, he should have a full and fair hearing before being finally settled with.

Can the people of Ontario, at least the many who are expressing themselves so unreservedly about their fellow-countrymen of whose blood Riel is, not conceive that there may be an honest division of feeling among these latter about Riel's cause?—that the cause which is

43

unfortunately championed by a man with his record may be in its way one that will deserve the sympathy of all Canadians in another generation, and that there is room for true feeling for it even now in the hearts of those most closely connected with its lonely supporters?

Do Ontario people really desire compatriots who could view unmoved the distress, the revolt, the bravery, the ruin and death of their blood relations, the half-breeds of the North-West, even in a bad cause, but *before* the half-breed excesses have been proved to be aught but the blindness or desperation of misguided men?

It is unfortunate that on account of the half-breeds Riel is too lightly thought of in Quebec, and that on account of Riel the half-breeds are damned in Ontario. Yet until Riel's trial is over, Riel should not be hanged, even in the latter Province.

Many of us have accepted and advertised sectional and hare-brained utterances as representative of French-Canadian feeling and have retorted with insult to a million and a half people who are our countrymen, and the descendants of men who shed as much of their blood for the Union Jack as ever did their English-speaking fellow-Canadians.

In the towns where the French-speaking Canadian comes still in contact with the charitable idea rampant about Waterloo-time that one Englishman is as good as three Frenchmen, he may become more or less bigoted himself. But there can scarcely be to my mind a peasantry anywhere in the world more simple, manly, hospitable and whole-souled than the French-Canadian habitants of the country districts.

I cannot realize that in any public question in the last few years in our country, French-speaking Canadians, when not apprehensive of aggression themselves, have been less patriotic, less loyal to the Dominion or less grasping than the English-speaking Canadians who outnumber them two to one, but who have in the Dominion Cabinet, which governs both races, ten representatives to the French-Canadian three.

Surely it is the sacred duty of every Canadian, whether French or English-speaking, to make the broadest allowance for the inborn prejudices of his neighbors of different tongue, to be sure that his own inborn prejudices are not his master.

"War and Mr. Meighen"

P.D. Ross and Arthur Meighen were personal friends, and comrades in the Conservative Party. The word "integrity" that so consistently attends Ross is nowhere so apt as in one major difference that arose between them. From his files I have an envelope bearing in Ross' writing "War and Mr. Meighen"—its contents I believe a bit of Canadian history as well as illumination on the lives of two renowned Canadians.

On Nov. 16, 1925, when he was Opposition Leader, Arthur Meighen astounded many by declaring in a speech at Hamilton, Ontario, that if he were returned to power in the next election, and if the British Empire were again to be involved in war, he would dissolve Parliament and hold a general election on the question whether Canada should enter the War. Just five days later, Ross wrote Meighen this letter:

Nov. 21st, 1925.

Hon. Arthur Meighen,
Parliament Buildings,
Ottawa, Ontario.

Dear Mr. Meighen:—

After some hesitation, I think it would be well to put myself on record concerning the view expressed by you at Hamilton, namely:

If ever the time should come when the spectre of 1914 should again appear I believe it would be best, not only that Parliament should be called, *but that the decision of the Government which, of course, would have to be given promptly, should be submitted to the judgment of the people at a general election before troops should leave our shores.*

My conviction is strong that the principle of representative government which has carried the English-speaking peoples along safely so far is contravened by the idea of holding a plebiscite, for a general election upon a single issue would be practically that in a moment of national crisis.

Without desiring to trouble you by argument, but to make my feeling clear, I think that to propose that a great national issue at an emergent time should be relegated to the judgment and delay of a great mass of individual voters, mostly ill informed, instead of having the decision made by representative and better informed men in Parliament, would ordinarily be to call for whatever opposition I might be able to give.

I feel obliged to keep silent at present, as far as public comment is concerned, the duty of the moment being I think to do nothing to hurt the possibility of this country getting back to an effective national policy industrially, but I want to be frank about the other matter at once, so that no misunderstanding can arise as to *The Journal*'s motives if comment should seem necessary at a later date.

Regretting very much that I feel it necessary to express dissent, I am with every regard,

Yours sincerely,
P.D. Ross

On December 4 Mr. Meighen replied from Ottawa:

Dear Mr. Ross,

It is to me a matter of very keen regret that you cannot agree with the terms of the speech I made at Hamilton. Another matter of regret to me is that I failed to discuss with you, before making the speech, this subject which as a matter of fact I have had under review for months. Until your letter arrived I was quite certain I had done so the time I visited your office some months ago. In this I must have been in error. Had I not been under that impression I certainly would have seen you before leaving to make the speech.

Circumstances which impelled me to make the statement rather sooner than I had otherwise intended will be disclosed to you later. Necessarily I could not make known what was in my mind widely for reasons that you can easily understand. I had discussed the subject though with quite a number of outstanding leaders of the Party, and especially with those who had to do with the conduct of this country through the late war. All with whom I discussed the subject agreed definitely and firmly with my position and were entirely convinced that the procedure which I advocated at Hamilton would be absolutely necessary in Canada in the event of another crisis arising.

May I emphasize this very important fact. What was advocated at Hamilton was not so much a policy, indeed not a policy at all, as regards Empire relations, but merely a procedure in order to give, in the best way, effect to a policy. Never would I swerve from the great principle that a Government must always assume its responsibility and in the event of a crisis involving the likelihood of war being upon us, must declare its stand and upon that stand must live or die. Nor do I think there are any who know me, or indeed any of the people of this country who would doubt that under circumstances involving peril to the Empire, any Government of which I may be the head will not hesitate to declare definitely for Canada taking the honourable part and adhering to that course.

What the Hamilton speech involves is this, that without subtracting in the least from Governmental responsibility which responsibility of course would involve the immediate making of preparations, mobilization under the existing law, and all other steps necessary to carry out the declared intention of the Administration, there should as a condition previous to the despatch of troops from our shores, be a submission of the Government's policy to the people in the regular constitutional form of a general election. This should not, and would not involve delay. In 1914 we could have had two general elections before troops were actually despatched. Had we done so I believe much of the disunion which afterwards developed would probably have been avoided.

In 1917 the crisis was even more perilous than at the outbreak of war. Had the Government at that time undertaken to enforce conscription even in the face of such a crisis without an appeal to the people there is no telling what might have happened to this country. In this Dominion we absolutely must have regard to the composition of our people. I feel absolutely certain that the very assurance of their being consulted, as can without great inconvenience be done, will have a steadying and quieting effect, and will tend rather to strengthen their faith in the fairness of their fellow citizens and predispose them to join with us in any necessary steps to secure our ultimate security and peace.

The talk about a surrender to Bourassa is utter nonsense. Such a mistake arises through confusing policy with procedures. As you will have observed Mr. Bourassa, just as I would have expected, has not accepted, but rather denounced the course to which I am committed.

Personally I believe very strongly that the peace of the world for many, many years, and probably for more than one generation, if not for many more, is now secure. In this belief the people of Canada I think generally share. Why then should we suffer that a large portion of our people remain longer in a state of utterly unnecessary apprehension to the very great detriment of our strength as a Party, and consequently our usefulness to the Dominion?

Some mistakes and misunderstanding have arisen by reason of small extracts being taken from my speech, rather than the entire references to the subject. I am attaching hereto copy of what was actually said.

In the above I have sought to express clearly and frankly my own mind on the subject, and I most earnestly hope these views do not diverge seriously from your own.

With kindest personal regards,

Yours very truly,
Arthur Meighen.

How much Mr. Meighen's speech contributed to his party's defeat in the General Election the following June, I can't guess. In the see-saw struggle between the Liberals and Conservatives at that juncture, every issue counted. Ross' anxiety about it boiled over at the Conservative Convention in Winnipeg in October, 1927, called to elect a successor to Meighen. R.B. Bennett was chosen, but Meighen made a major address in defence of his speech that provoked Ontario's Premier Ferguson to such vehement disagreement he said he would quit the party if Meighen's "election-before-war" scheme were supported.

Ross was out there, writing daily signed pieces for *The Journal*. He wrote that Meighen's appeal was "dramatic, splendid in form and fire, eloquent, and towards its close poignant and touching. Beyond all doubt it won the sympathy of a majority of the delegates." However, it "might bring an ugly and perhaps fatal clash for the party between delegates." "Mr. Meighen's outcry was little better than one of wounded vanity."

Ross did not allude to his having written Meighen, and he saw to it that *The Journal* published almost the full text of Meighen's address. Yet the following day on the front page he wrote a signed apology:

> . . . I come now to a wrong I have done to the Canadian public man just named, the Hon. Arthur Meighen. In a previous despatch I ascribed his onslaught upon the Conservative convention as due to "little better than wounded vanity" because many political and personal friends had refused to agree to his famous Hamilton speech. I should not have used the word vanity. It was a mean thing to say of a man with the great public record and achievement of Mr. Meighen. It was written in heat and haste and in apprehension of a great evil in the convention and Canada. I beg to withdraw it and apologize for it. Perhaps "wounded feeling" would have been fair. The rest of what I said stands.

That was P.D. Ross, all right.

To "Mitch," with Scorn

For lesser politics, Ross had less patience. Consider his dismissal of Mitchell Hepburn who in June 1934 was Leader of the Opposition in the Ontario Legislature:

> Apart from gross misstatements of fact, Mr. Hepburn has launched a continuous series of assertions about public men and public affairs which are unworthy of any public man dealing with his fellow Canadians. He has promulgated to the best of his voluminous vituperation the idea that everybody opposed to him politically is dishonest. He has made assertions and promises which may be characterized as hardly less than crazy about the amount of expenditure he will cut down, the offices he will abolish, the civil servants he will dismiss if he gets into power. The Government employees he will chuck out, he tells us, will look like an Orange Parade on the Twelfth of July. In the Liberal behalf

in the Province, and of course in his own, Mr. Hepburn is a whirlwind of misrepresentation and impossible abuse. Perhaps the way he puts it to himself is in the words of an ancient Greek poet, "God is not averse to deceit in a holy cause."

About "Capital L" Liberalism
He had often a buccaneering touch in his political editorials, you seemed to hear him chuckling as he went into the fray. The Beauharnois scandal in 1931 was for him clear proof of his worst suspicions of the Liberal Party. He lit into them hard on that, but on one occasion paused beforehand to scoff at the support *The Citizen* was giving the Government on the issue. *The Citizen* was but "caddying" to its latest patrons; "Among the afflictions of this country are four-flush radicals; one of the worst, among the most hypocritical, is *The Ottawa Citizen.*" That matter dismissed, he went on to argue that Mackenzie King in retaining silence on the matter had allowed his party and its moneyed friends—"certain financial mandarins"—to permit exploitation of a great national water resource, "to build up fabulous wealth for themselves at the people's expense."

And then the characteristic swing:

The truth is that "Liberalism," so far as it is a label for certain Canadian politicians, is a fraud. There must be thousands of real Liberals in Canada who are shamed by such betrayals. Many of them who must be thinking today in the famous phrase of Gilbert Keith Chesterton: "As much as I ever did, more than I ever did, I believe in Liberalism; but there was a rosy time of innocence when I believed in Liberals."

A Blow for Capitalism
In other moods Ross would seem a painstaking teacher, trying once and for all to set forth the facts and dimensions of some major subject. On February 1, 1935, he gathered class together, so to speak, to let them get this business of socialism and communism straight. His editorial began with a quotation from J.S. Woodsworth, then leader of the C.C.F. party which was the father of today's New Democratic Party. "I do not think capitalism can go on much longer," Woodsworth had said. Then:

Please note from the dictionaries that it is not necessary to use the word money to indicate either capital or wealth. Money is capital. Capital is not money, except to about the millionth part of an inch. Capital is property. Capital may include money; but for every piece of coined money in the world, there is a million times as much value of property—all of which is capital.

Capital is simply the surplus product of human labor. Everything that any human being owns or possesses is capital, except his skin.

When Mr. Woodsworth says he does not think capitalism can go on much longer, he appears to have a pessimistic idea that the moment has almost arrived when the earth and its people shall be destroyed by some cataclysm—when

The cloud-capp'd towers, the gorgeous palaces.
The solemn temples, the great globe itself,
Yea, all which it inherit shall dissolve
And like an insubstantial pageant faded,
Leave not a rack behind.

For all civilization is capital, and nothing on earth but capitalism of some kind is possible while Earth lasts.

Let us take the case of, say a carpenter with a saw. The saw is capital. Using that and other tools, also capital, the carpenter manages not only to live but to save a little money. He buys a small home. Perhaps now, being a responsible citizen, he is able to get some small contract for carpenter work. He makes a profit. He gets a bigger contract. It succeeds. He finds himself with quite a little money on hand. He knows all about carpenters' saws, so he decides to set-up a small saw factory. It succeeds; and by and by he builds a bigger factory, makes a good deal of money, buys a bigger house for his family, is able to invest money in bank stock and gets on the Board of Directors of a Bank. Behold now another bloated capitalist.

The Communistic idea, and to some extent the Socialistic idea, is to divide up the ex-carpenter's capital; and people who own anything have to listen to such talk because, alas, in these modern days when anybody denounces capital and wants that everything that anybody else has should be divided up, it is no longer etiquette to bash his head in.

What Mr. Woodsworth and his fellow Socialists really aim to attack, although many of them muffle up their own intelligence in vague blather about "capital," is not capital but the evil which is done by some of the uses of capital, or of the power which capital gives. A vast amount of such evil is certainly done by greedy or unscrupulous individuals who have come to possess large capital—and even more by greedy and soulless wealthy and powerful corporations. This is not the fault of capital. It begins in the fault of much human nature. It continues in the failure of the rest of us to check it. Whenever a human being or beings have obtained unchecked or overwhelming power, that power has been liable to be misused. This has been the cause of innumerable wars, the cause of endless political oppressions, the cause often of social oppressions, the historic story of reckless and brutal crime in high places. Therefore, unchecked power should not be tolerated by mankind; it should be fought wherever it appears, whether in connection with capital or anything else. To this extent, the Socialists are right and commendable. But when they preach the abolition of capital, rather than the smashing as far as possible of the evil which sometimes attaches to the possession or exercise of capital, they are as wise as the man who cried for the moon, or the other man who proposed to cut off a neighbor's legs because the neighbor might possibly walk into a bear trap.

But the socialists held Ross in great respect. He had on occasion taken Labor's side as stoutly as he had taken employers' side. They knew he had declined the post of Lieutenant Governor of Ontario lest it confine his freedom to fight as he wished. Indeed, Mr. Woodsworth—a man of singular honor—would probably have written much the same letter when Ross turned 90 as did his successor. M.J. Coldwell as party leader expressed "appreciation for the work you have done for this community and for our country over such a long period of time" and thanked him for his many "kindly references to the work that we (in our party) believe we are doing sincerely for the good of the country which we both love and try to serve in our respective ways."

52

"I Love Animals"

Yet the mind and writing of P.D. Ross were not boxed in by politics and economics. He wrote about "most anything", about boyhood, hobbies, poetry; he wrote of friends, of the beauty of outdoors and the fun and reward in sport.

At a time when hunting was all the rage he was taken out with friends to a camp north of Sudbury and he shot a moose. In "A Moose" he wrote of that deed:

> It was a magnificent young bull moose, larger than an average horse, weighing probably a thousand pounds. What could we do with it? We could take only a small portion of the meat—which we did. The spread of horns was not great enough to make the head worth serious trouble. The hide would have been heavy, and as regards carrying either meat, horns or hide, our canoe was down to the limit of safety already.
>
> The morning was one of the glorious ones of the late Canadian autumn. The magnificent, beautiful animal lay there in the rich sunlight, amid the autumn glory of the woods, its powerful life gone. We went away, leaving the splendid thing to rot.
>
> I have not killed anything since, for sport.

I remember once as a young reporter going out the front door of *The Journal* in rather a rush, probably for the two reasons that often motivated me as a reporter: I was late, and I was looking forward to what I was about to do. Ross, about to come in the door, was obliged to yield. "Where are you off to so gaily, young fellow?" I told him I was going to cover the Richmond Fall Fair. "Ah, good," he said; and then, speaking quickly so as not to detain me but with instant sincerity, "see you spend a lot of time with the animals; I love animals, but I've never taken the time really to know them, which I regret—except these fellows." With the last phrase he pointed down to the Fox Terrier who daily accompanied him on his walk to the office and remained at his desk until he left. A long succession of terriers brought gladness to Mr. and Mrs. Ross, and the pride of the elevator man was that all of them learned, despite occasional deliberate misleading coaxing, which floor was the Chief's and wouldn't budge at other than the sixth floor.

One day Mr. Ross wrote an editorial entitled "Just a Dog." It began this way:

An item in *The Journal* one morning told of the Ottawa Blue Cross Hospital having had 145 stray dogs in refuge during the year.

One thought of one's own, if listed among stray dogs. Stray dogs! Bundles of misery, of pathos, of hope! Living things each of which has looked upon some human being as a god. Anxious eyes, trembling tails! Just dogs.

They are nuisances enough at times, dogs. They bark, they fight, they get dirty and paw you, they stray, they get stolen, they eat garbage. But if you come to analyze their faults, you find that their faults come most of them from affection and from loyalty. In the dog's mind abides the conviction that he has to champion his master and protect his master's property, and ought to be vociferous about it, and that above all, anybody else's dog has to be kept in his place.

Thrash him, and he makes love to you the moment it is over. Ignore him, and he waits humbly and anxiously for your kinder mind. His greatest joy in life is to be your comrade, and he has a dominant idea throughout his brief existence that everything his master does is wonderful, and that a dog should always be on hand to show complete admiration.

A dog is not long-lived. So it was written, long ago, that "It is the inevitable tragedy of the life of every lover of dogs that his heart shall be a place of ghosts."

. . . And Poetry Too

Sport and journalism and service to his community released his energy and power, but poetry was in his mind and heart; now shyly, now clamorously so that he wanted to pass on its secret to friend and stranger. In the 21 years I was on the paper "with" him (his age from 70 to 91) the greater part of his writing was not editorials but perceptive and vigorous reviews of books, mostly of poetry. He knew many of the then most-honored Canadian poets personally, several very well, such as Archibald Lampman and Duncan Campbell Scott. He helped many a Canadian poet financially; many a hopeful poetry association, though they didn't all survive. The interesting thing was that this rugged athlete, dressed usually with immaculate wing collar, was most susceptible to the lyricists of love and human kindness and the soft touch of evening. Of this strain in him he once said: "When I was a small boy I wanted to be a poet. I remember that it was a cruel blow to me when one of my sisters told me I didn't look like a poet. Nevertheless I wrote a lot of poems, but somehow or other I got steered into an Engineering course. . . ."

In a sense he applied an engineer's eye to poetry, a much exercised hobby of his being to prove by arithmetic that the best poets used the shortest words!

"An analysis of the whole of the great poetry of our language would find possibly 4 or 5 per cent of words of more than two syllables, about 15 or 16 per cent of words of two syllables, 80 per cent of words of one syllable."

Imagine making this the whole subject of an address to the Canadian National Exhibition Press Day, in 1937! English, he said, was the most simple, direct and compact of the present languages of civilization. An American philologian had found that of 40 languages the English version Gospel of St. Mark could be translated into the least number of syllables. English took 29,000 syllables to do the job, whereas the average for all the Teutonic languages was 32,650, the Slav group 36,500, the Latin group 40,200, the Indo-Iranian group 43,100, French 36,000.

"We need not be surprised," said Mr. Ross, "for the Gospel of Mark deals chiefly with the things of the spirit; and it is with the things of the spirit that the English language deals best."

Without texts he quoted dozens of passages, sometimes giving four or five verses from a poem, but the short ones will show what he was driving at:

Wordsworth:
> Will no one tell me what she sings?
> Perhaps the plaintive numbers flow
> For old, unhappy, far-off things,
> And battles long ago;

Shakespeare:
> Fear no more the heat o' the sun.

Burns:
> I'm wearin' awa, John
> Like snaw wreaths in thaw, John,
> I'm wearin' awa
> To the Land o' the Leal. . . .

Tennyson:
> Sunset and evening star,
> And one clear call for me,
> And may there be no moaning of the bar
> When I put out to sea.

John McRae:
> We are the dead. Short days ago,
> We lived, felt dawn, saw sunsets glow,
> Loved and were loved—and now we lie
> In Flanders fields.

The statistics he gave?

In Shakespeare's "Dirge of Cymbeline," 112 words in all, there are 88 words of one syllable.

In Coleridge's *The Ancient Mariner*, there are among the more than 3,000 words about 60 words of more than two syllables, including many hyphenates—just two per cent.

In Kipling's "Danny Deever," apart from the word "regiment" inevitable in a soldiers' ballad, there is but a single word of more than two syllables among the 300 words.

Ross' second address on this hobby, "Canadian Poets and the Short Word," was broadcast for the C.B.C. on Feb. 12, 1938. Let's consider three:

Isabella Valancey Crawford:
> O if Love build on sparkling sea,
> And if Love build on golden strand,
> And if Love build on rosy cloud,
> To Love, these are the solid land.

Audrey Alexandra Brown: (of a brother who died in the war)
  Ah, youth is sweet upon the lips!—the wine of life is good,
  He poured that wine with steadfast hands one day in Ypres wood—
  Let it forget him if it may, the land that gave him birth
  There is a glory where he lies in green though alien earth.

Pauline Johnson: (whose father was chief of the Six Nations Indians)
  Sailing into the cloud land, sailing into the sun
  Into the crimson portals, ajar when life is done,
  O dear, dead race, my spirit too
  Would fain sail westward unto you.

Ross remarked at the end of several particularly long quotations that he had trained himself to put poetry to memory partly because he loved poetry and partly "from the hope that it might improve my own writing." And he had become familiar with the great and simple language of the Bible "because my father and mother, stout Scottish Presbyterians, had seen to it that I read a lot of the Bible."

I might add that I learned the hard way of his knowledge of the Bible. He had written an article using a small quote from the Bible which I thought was wrong. On the way to check the quote in the Library I chanced to meet him in the hall. Probably to show off, I asked him right then whether I might change his quote, telling him what I thought it should be. He looked at me kindly and said quietly: "Yes, Norman, I guess that's Luke, I used Matthew."

His Newspaper Principles
What did P.D. Ross feel about a newspaper, its role in community and country? What was his way? Why did he stand out? Over the decades he did set down his creed of what a paper should be about. I shall "lift" parts from various of his articles and talks, so to group ideas and avoid duplication:

On Responsibility
(To a convention in Ottawa, June 10, 1922, of Canada's weekly newspapers.)

There is the responsibility which newspapers owe to the public-spirited citizenship and to all good causes; and there is the responsibility which newspaper publishers owe to their own livelihood, and that of their employes.

A newspaper must exist if it is to do any good of any kind. There is an old saying that a living ass is better than a dead lion. Maybe so, maybe not, but at all events a dead lion can't do anything and neither can a dead newspaper. To live, a newspaper must please the public, or a sufficient part of it. A newspaper business is a commercial attempt, primarily, just as a butcher shop. It has to live as a business before it can do any good as an educator or an apostle. In short, the newspapers have to look out for number one, in an honorable way of course, before they look out for the public. This compels in newspapers both a vigorous pursuit of news and a limitation of their enthusiasms for the unlimited breadth of the public's enthusiasms.

A newspaper publisher should conduct his newspaper as he would conduct himself personally as a gentleman, using that word in its highest sense. This principle should cover the whole ground, but it might be added that a newspaper should be anxiously honest in its presentation of news; should give it fairly; should give it impartially, should give it mercifully. The aim should be to promote good causes and public advantage.

If in the course of public affairs a newspaper should find or think it finds public wrong or injustice or dishonesty, it should expose it even at the risk of loss or libel. The newspaper should be fair to other people's opinions, and be ready to give them every reasonable latitude in its columns. The publisher should not use his newspaper for mean or small-minded purposes, nor allow it to be so used. He should do what he can to promote mutual toleration and kindly feeling among all classes of his own people, and, more than that, among all countries and races of the world.

Sometimes a newspaper will find itself mistaken and doing injustice. It should make the thing right in the fullest and frankest possible way. Carelessness is no excuse. A newspaper has no right to hurt anyone's feelings, except perhaps unavoidably in the necessary promotion of some public cause.

If a newspaper's statement has been unjustifiable, it must make the most complete and unreserved amend possible, whether legal proceedings are threatened or not; it should apologize fully and humbly without regard to professional pride, and cheerfully pay any damage that can be fairly estimated. And this should be done not as a matter of apprehension of any consequences, but because the publisher owes it to himself as a decent citizen.

On Playing Fair Politics
(The 100th birthday celebration of the Brockville *Recorder*, January 16, 1921.)

I am told that the *Recorder* has always been of Grit persuasion. I do not admire this fact as much as I admire the *Recorder*'s age. I am not of the Grit persuasion myself, and I would like to feel a private hope that some day if I wire to the Hon. George Graham (the *Recorder's* publisher) that he ought really to come over to my side of politics, he will reply as an old-time journalist once did to a personal appeal from Sir John Macdonald: "It's a damned sharp curve, but I suppose we can make it."

There is one respect in which we newspapermen have fallen most from grace. It is the political respect, or rather I should say the partisan respect. There is where we have been most liable to be unfair, most liable to be bitter, most liable to be untruthful. "Three devils infest our newspaper offices," a prominent Canadian journalist said to me once, "the printer's devil, the careless devil and the political (partisan) devil, and of these three the worst is the political devil."

This might be illustrated by a story of the temper in which Jones dealt with Smith when the two neighbors fell out about Smith's cat.

Smith's cat had created a whole lot of trouble between the two neighbors resulting in an angry feud. But by and by the cat died. Smith thought an opportunity had come to make friends with Jones again. So he wrote Jones a polite note saying: "Mr. Smith sends his compliments to Mr. Jones and begs to say that his old cat died this morning."

Mr. Jones replied: "Mr. Jones is sorry to hear of Mr. Smith's trouble, but he had not heard that Mrs. Smith was ill."

That's the sort of temper we have maintained in newspaper offices, about political parties. Perhaps we will be all right in that respect in another hundred years.

As earnest of what he was saying, note the conclusion to that address:

I beg to propose the health of the *Recorder*, accompanying with it the name of Hon. George Graham, a Canadian who has played a great public part in this country, and who, if the fortune of war should again place the Liberal party in power at Ottawa, I venture to hope to see again one of the chief ministers of the government.

About Editorials
(An address in Kitchener at the time of the Diamond Jubilee of the Kitchener *Record*.)

Ross often said the editorial page was the most important of a newspaper: "the outstanding glory of any journal is to create, to correct, to guide and mould public opinion." As President of The Canadian Daily Newspaper Association, attending the jubilee celebration, he gave these views about editorials.

For millions of people the daily newspaper is the only university, the only source of information, the chief fountain of their thoughts, their judgments, their prejudices, their attitude towards life.

The newspaper, if it is to perform a proper public service, must try to amplify, to explain, to interpret the news, to give the news behind the news. There is a difference between news and truth. News signalizes an event, truth reveals the facts and causes underlying that event.

That is why newspapers have their editorial page.

About editorial pages, and editorials, there is a great deal of misconception. There are some who think that the business of an editorial page is to make itself the unwavering supporter of a political party; or the custodian of all causes; or the champion of all grievances; or a type of journalistic pulpit for sermonising. They would have editorial pages crusading constantly for this thing or that.

On the other hand, there are those who profess to despise editorials, who will tell you that such and such an editorial represents merely the opinions of some individuals that no reason exists why the opinion of this individual should be more authoritative or more impressive than the opinion of anybody else.

All of these conceptions are wrong.

A newspaper editorial page, if it is to be honest, if it is to maintain its influence, cannot simply be the mouthpiece, the mere voice of a political party. It may give allegiance to the policies and principles of a party; may support honestly and vigorously the platform of a party. But it cannot, if it is to put the truth first, or the public good first, support always and consistently the acts of a political organization. After all, there is a vast difference between a political party's principles and policies and the acts of the men who, for the time being, may be in charge of the party's conduct.

Nor can a newspaper editorial page take it upon itself to dictate individual conduct, or to sermonise or exhort the public day after day. Continual nagging will weaken its power when the day comes for bold words.

The function of the newspaper is to present and interpret facts fairly; to support all good causes to the best of its ability, to fight wrongs or rank injustice, to try as best it may to create an attitude of correct and just thought in the community.

Above all, a newspaper must be fair to those who disagree with it, must avoid unnecessary vituperation, abuse and personalities.

May I be pardoned for using as an illustration a newspaper with which I am proud to have been associated for many years.

The editorials in *The Ottawa Journal*, like the editorials in any newspaper, no matter who may actually write them, are not the snap opinions or verdicts of some particular individual. They are shaped by a consciousness of the paper's history, of its public responsibility, of the story and tradition behind it.

The individual writer of an editorial—the theme and aim of which may have been decided upon after discussion of all the relevant facts, and perhaps after consultation with some authority upon the particular subject to be discussed—does not follow merely his own private prejudices or views, or air lightly his own opinions.

He writes with a consciousness of his own responsibility to his newspaper. That is why we speak of "the paper's" editorials, not of the editorials of a particular writer. And that is why editorials as distinct from special articles are anonymous, and why I am of the opinion they should be.

(As a footnote to that, may I say his successors sought hard to live up to his views about editorials. For years, *The Journal* had been the most quoted editorial page in Canada, and it was cheering to E.N.S., to Grattan and then to me as editors, that our editorials continued to hold that position in the impartial count of the Canadian Press Clipping Bureau.)

Has a Paper Got Problems!
(Address to The Canadian Club of Montreal, Jan. 23, 1933.)

At the outset of this speech, "The Inside of a Newspaper," Ross repeated his theory that "a newspaper should mean well, but if it carries that idea too far it won't live long," and then described the mess of problems a paper had to confront if it was to survive!

Do not make any mistakes about the precise and meticulous nature of production. Your newspaper is printed from stereotyped plates, of which some twenty to forty have to be made and placed on a newspaper press successively each day. We have three editions in the afternoon and three in the morning. Each of these editions necessitates the changing of many plates on the presses—in the case of the morning paper of all the plates. Thus you have every week day in the year seven regular press starts. How many times during the past two years, during which there have been 2,500 press starts, do you suppose a *Journal* press has started as much as one minute late? Twice in two years. On July 10 there was a break in one of the presses, and the morning paper started seven minutes late. On February 3, 1932, one of the evening editions started two minutes late. There was no satisfactory reason and there was a row about it.

I would like you to realize what a remarkable thing newspaper accuracy is. Something happens, let us say a motor accident. A reporter writes it. There's the first chance of error. The reporter's story, when written, goes to a revising copy reader, who generally condenses the story. There's the second chance. From the copy reader the story goes to the typesetter. There's another chance of error. From the linotype machine the story goes to the proofreader. He looks it over for mistakes, and corrects them—but perhaps he makes a mistake himself in doing so. That's another chance of error. Then the story goes to the assembling tables to be put into what we call "chases," which are steel frames the size of a newspaper page. More chance of error by misplacing lines. After the page has been made up in the chase it has to be taken to the stereotyping room to have a plate made from it in semi-circular form, to be clamped on a cylinder of the printing press—more chance of mistake. So, every statement or item runs through ten chances of mistake. Usually more than 1,000 such items appear daily. If each runs ten chances of mistake there have been at least ten thousand chances of some sort of error.

Of course things will occur. There is an illustrative story of an American paper welcoming the return to town of an officer who had been wounded in the face in the war. A big headline ran "Return of Battle-Scared Hero." Next day the paper corrected the mistake. It explained that the headline should have read: "Return of Bottle-Scarred Hero."

Once there was a vice-regal ball in Ottawa. *The Journal*'s description of the dress of Mrs. B., the wife of one of my valued friends who was then a cabinet minister, was this: "Mrs. B. was attired in a beautiful dress of crepe de chine, trimmed by two bathtubs and a toilet." There had been a formal opening the same day of a new public bath in Ottawa, and in the correction of misprints a line from the bath story had been transposed into the story of the vice-regal ball. The Minister dropped me a note to say that he could have tolerated the bathtub.

As to a newspaper's having to cater to its readers, Mr. Ross had a little fun and lots of sense:

A newspaper must first of all be a successful business enterprise. Most of you are quite ready to go ahead cheerfully and unconsciously trying to make every newspaper an unsuccessful enterprise. The theory of most of you here is, I am sure, that a newspaper ought to be conducted in a very dignified, high class and educational way. Each of you of course when he picks up the paper pounces first upon the latest murder or scandal—but each of you is anxious to see every newspaper trying to improve the morals of the rest of the community.

I am not arguing that any newspaper has any pretext to be yellow or to be low, or to be recklessly sensational or to seek to cater to either the weaknesses or the prejudices of the community. I am stating that the newspaper to live must look anxiously to please as many different sorts of people as possible.

Hooray for Comics!

Ross was in favor of comics, no ifs and ands about it! He suspected that in popular following Mutt and Jeff ran ahead of editorials, news and even sport. In 1909 at a meeting of the Ottawa Women's Teachers' Association, it was decided to ask the papers to exercise more care in the choice of comics. P.D. met the challenge head-on:

"*The Journal* cannot do that; for all possible care is exercised already. *The Journal* has the best selection of these features which is possible in America. A great deal of innocent fun in life seems to arouse antagonism in some natures merely because it is fun. Other temperaments are prone to think that every human interest is questionable unless it be of some direct utility—a horrible world that would make, surely. *The Journal* is under the impression that to cut off its comic supplement would be to destroy an amount of innocent pleasure in Ottawa homes, which would be a blunder almost as bad as a crime.''

A Chastened Advertiser

There is still afoot some opinion that newspapers will cut their cloth to suit the advertiser. Let's close this review of Ross' thoughts about newspapers with this piece from his book *Retrospects*:

Tom Lindsay, alias Thos. Lindsay & Co., used to have one of the largest department stores in Ottawa.

Tom Lindsay was a live wire, who did not limit himself to merchandise. In 1906 he conceived the idea of taking a hand in the electric situation in Ottawa.

Charter after charter had been granted by the city council to electric companies in Ottawa up to that date, with the uniform result that after each new charter there was amalgamation of the new with the old: and so a continual increase of capital burden upon electric service in the city.

The Journal in consequence was opposing the granting of new charters by the City Council. When Tom Lindsay headed for another charter, *The Journal* opposed his proposition. Mr. Lindsay's scheme was to dig a power canal from Britannia to below the Deschenes rapids on the Ottawa. As the argument grew warm, *The Journal* rather suggested that Mr. Lindsay was more likely to sell out his charter if he got it than to really go ahead himself.

Mr. Lindsay didn't like that. He caused an intimation to be sent along that if *The Journal* didn't shut up, he would take away his advertising.

He was the largest advertiser we had, except one other.

The Journal kept on, but the city council didn't mind. They gave Mr. Lindsay a charter for the Metropolitan Electric Co.

Shortly afterwards a prominent citizen of Ottawa, long since dead, who had been more or less associated with Mr. Lindsay in the application for the Metropolitan charter, came into *The Journal* office. He had quarrelled with Mr. Lindsay. He produced a photograph of a private letter written by Mr. Lindsay to Mr. J.R. Booth offering to sell the Metropolitan charter to Mr. Booth for $20,000.

We had a cut made of the photograph and published it in *The Journal*.

Mr. Lindsay next day ordered his advertisement out of the paper.

The contract of Thos. Lindsay & Co. was for a quarter page at the left top of one of the pages of *The Journal*.

A day later the quarter page was left entirely blank and white in *The Journal* except for a couple of lines which were inserted in the centre of the space in the smallest type we had, as follows:

This space for sale
Formerly owned by
T. Lindsay.

The above appeared daily for two or three days. Most everybody knew what it meant.

Tom Lindsay was a good sport, after his first fury. A message came from him:

Take that d— thing out of the paper. I am sending copy for advertisement as usual.

A Few Personal Touches

From his own words I hope the reader has sensed the personality of this man, but may I offer a few personal glimpses of it? Having just read his defence of comics and that bluff-calling spoof saying Lindsay's ad space was for sale reminds me that one who knew him well asserts that if he and his wife ever had any fun, "it was purely inadvertently." I wonder about that. He did not pose as a wit. The "jokes" he told were recollections of people and events he found amusing, not out of jokebooks; he was not at home with idle chat and so some were frightened by his silence. Yet I've gathered that if their lives and natures were not fun, they were full of good humor and happy activity. In the early days of street cars they'd get on one on a summer evening and ride to the end of the line, she in a long dress with parasol and picture hat. At home they'd read aloud to one another, including what some might call light trash. They were crossword puzzle fans and bridge players, though I gather he was more reckless than skilled at bridge. I chanced upon them one time in their boathouse laughing to kill themselves because P.D. had upset the picnic hamper and inadvertently shoved the dog in the water to keep him from the sandwiches.

It seems he liked to laugh with, rather than at. A favorite one-liner of his was from a skit his father wrote him in a letter telling of a visitor to *The Journal* in the 'nineties going into the news room and asking if the editor was in. A disenchanted man at a desk looked up and said, "Some of them are." P.D. was the world's worst and fastest driver and a regular recipient of police tickets; he put them to use one year by adding up what he had paid and sending a cheque for ten times that amount to the Policemen's Ball, or whatever it was. When some friend or important citizen would come in to ask that his name be kept out of the paper because he had been fined, P.D. would reach into his side drawer and hand him Journal clippings of police court items saying P.D. Ross had been fined for speeding. "We run all traffic offenders in this paper," he'd roar with a laugh, "serves 'em right."

I think P.D. saw life as a whole, and I think that calls for a sense of humor. Panhandlers lay in wait for him in the depression years and he almost never disappointed them, giving them not only some silver but laughing orders to stay out of the tavern. On another level of giving, Mrs. Ross' nurse-companion Florence McConnell once told me P.D. and his wife spent many happy hours poring over ways to put their money to the best use in helping the poor, the sick and the underprivileged—including $350,000 to the Perley Home for Incurables. "You'd never believe the parade of benevolent and charity organizations that comes to this house for advice and money and they all get one or the other—and a lot of time."

Stanley Lewis, the Mayor of Ottawa, put this very well in an official letter to Ross on his 90th birthday. I shall quote just two paragraphs, though the whole letter was full of warm insight: "As one remembers the past, and as one has heard of it, there have been few things of public benefit to which you have not given your generous help, and never conspicuously unless the cause needed your own support. Indeed it is almost betraying a confidence to say this for I am in a favored position to know of such things, but your policy in this regard is so opposite to that of men who avoid 'doing good by stealth' that I trust I may mention it for the purpose of expressing respect for it. Ottawa in so many things owes you so much that it is impossible to list the ways. Many of them are not known, many of them may be forgotten, but each of them has made your city a better place. . . . I wish this were not your ninetieth birthday. I wish it were your fiftieth, or your fortieth or your thirtieth. It would be a fine thing to look forward to the lifetime of a man who is by nature a nobleman, and by intelligence a servant of the people not a dictator, and by culture a scholarly master of the art of living."

I add two personal recollections of the sort of kindness many in *The Journal* knew from him. I had in those years, and still have, a back and neck that go out of sorts from time to time. In 1947, he was rarely in his office and I longed to slip in and lie flat on his long couch once in a while for 15 minutes, as the doctor had advised. I sent him a four-line note explaining the nuisance and asking him whether I might occasionally use it when he was not in. In no time at all a note came back, which I treasure:

> Dear Norman—Make yourself at home any time, and whether I'm there or not. When I deceive myself with the idea that I'm busy I don't hear or see.

A month or so later, when I had to stay away for a week or more he wrote me:

> Indulge yourself freely as regards health; there is no reason for any neglect. On my 21st birthday I made some good resolutions and one of them was that my physical vigor would be a A-No. 1 consideration with me—that I would never allow a day to pass without some sort of exercise, if only a sharp half-hour's walk. I've kept that resolution. I'm writing from the depths of the worst snow storm my 89 years have seen. No motor car has passed my front door for two days. Haven't been able to get anyone out—haven't been able to get out myself!
>
> Regards to your lady, Yrs,
P.D.R.

The third recollection is more significant, relating not just to me but to the future of *The Journal*.

Not long after the war he came into my room, moved quickly to the only guest chair and said "I'd like to talk to you." It was the only time he ever sat down in my office.

"I don't think we have enough news of finance and business in the paper. Out at the golf club yesterday C.D. Howe and others were talking of the great changes coming in Canada. The State will enter more and more into our lives. The big projects and advanced techniques that business and industry had to develop in the war years will make it hard for the corner grocer or little fellow in anything to survive. As a paper we will have to watch that trend and report on it, for it will affect all people and our whole economy. It will be big government versus big business. It's too bad, but maybe only big business can stand up against big government."

He fell silent for a moment and looked out towards Parliament and the Gatineau Hills, then: "You're going to see big changes; and newspapers will have to change too, with better plant and equipment and reserves, and that costs money. I've always said a paper's first duty was to make money, *if it goes bust all its other duties are irrelevant.*"

The last words came out with a kind of laughing shout as he rose to go, the way he ended many talks. He paused at the door: "But don't worry about that, Norman, just keep your mind on putting out a good paper."

I had the feeling he had intended to say more. I had known that before and during the war P.D. and E.N.S. had discussed seriously the chances of *The Journal* standing independently against the Southam group paper and a good French language paper in a city as small as Ottawa. They had allowed several would-be buyers to make preliminary examination of the paper's affairs. I believe the old gentleman came in to give me the drift of his thinking. It was yet another example of the subtle sensitivity he felt for the problems of others, of which Mayor Lewis had written.

Heartbreak

Far the most moving revelation of the inner nature of P.D. Ross had come to me some years earlier when he suffered the first real setback and heartbreak of his life. Mrs. Ross died Dec. 8, 1943. She was 77 and he then 85. They had been married since 1891, without the blessing of children but in abiding happiness, though Mrs. Ross' poor health over many years kept her much to her home and herself, save for his company.

I hope not in poor taste, I use a confidential memo I wrote in pencil on copy paper now blear, addressed to my father and Grattan O'Leary. Mr. Ross had called me to his home just a few days after the funeral, and we were all worried about his own health. This was the memo:

It was 3:00 Thursday afternoon when I went. A parlor maid showed me into his library and he rose to greet me, rather more slowly than he used to but to his full height. We chatted about the weather a bit, it had been well below zero every day of the week.

"Yes," he said, "these have been cold days."

He thought for a while and got up to put another stick on the fire, sat down, squared his great shoulders and looked straight into my eyes and it seemed almost through me:

"I am taking advantage of your offer to help me, Norman. Would you look after sending the 300 odd cards of thanks to all our friends. I'm afraid I am unable. It is a big job and you may want to get help."

I told him I would not need help and we went at once into the details of the work.

"You know, I'm told there are 90 direct relatives of my mother and father, and I'm afraid I've lost track of them. Mrs. Ross knew them better than I."

He stopped talking and I thought it better to keep the silence. After a few minutes he looked up from the fire and began again, quietly, without any "dramatics."

"She was a wonderful woman. She had a broad, comprehending mind. Whatever I interested myself in she was able to be interested in and to talk helpfully to me about. I guess no two people have ever been given such happiness, such a successful relationship. We always had ample means, usually more than we needed. We travelled all over the world together. I believe with two exceptions of about a month we were never apart."

Again he stopped talking for a few minutes, looking through the fire, his hands firmly grasping the ends of the chair arms. His books were around him on all the walls; his university diplomas, his sporting trophies and pictures. But he looked only into the fire, and the cold winter sun did little but throw a white ray of light across the floor.

"By God's mercy, though," resumed Mr. Ross, raising his voice a little, I think to keep it from faltering, "she was herself right to the end. By God's mercy."

"The last six years she has had to stay in the house we have been even more together and read greatly together with deep pleasure. On the day before she died I was with her in the morning. She wasn't feeling too badly and we chatted. After lunch I believe she went to sleep and I guess she stayed more or less asleep from then on. The nurses wouldn't waken her in the afternoon but at about 10:30 I went in to her bedroom to say goodnight. I kissed her, but I don't remember whether we spoke or not. My mind is not very clear these days. Then about 2:00 the next morning she died, and they called me."

His voice was soft, and he looked very, very tired. But the tears of a few days earlier had either been cried out or controlled.

Mr. Ross suddenly pointed to a briefcase. It was the work I was to take away. I moved at once, but then he started to talk again, I think feeling a little guilty of his sudden pointing to the case. He was thanking me for having come and I said all of us at the office had been thinking of him and with hope we would see him around again soon. I suggested it might be helpful to him if he were to get at a little work, some editorial. He said yes, and then talked of possibly visiting his niece, Mrs. Gerald Birks in Nassau. "I don't want to go any place I have been with Mrs. Ross. And I don't want to go any place Mrs. Ross hasn't been to. But I may go to Nassau."

He talked a little while about the loyalty of his friends in *The Journal* and of his staff at his home, specially Miss Florence McConnell who had been a companion to Mrs. Ross for 14 years. Then he rose, slowly, and insisted on accompanying me to the door. It was cold in the outer hall as I put on my overshoes, but he would not heed my request he go inside. "I must have the constitution of a horse. I don't feel any great physical shock, but I'm sick in mind and heart."

He shook my hand, and closed the door very gently as I came away. Picking my steps along the snow-drifted walk I thought . . . "And some think he is austere."

He Grows Older

Ross did go to Nassau for a short while, but thereafter he remained in Ottawa. He played a little bridge, saw something of older friends who were still about, came to the office a little, walked in the Sandy Hill area of his home—and read: mostly he read. But he never became a grouch or a moper. At a party on his 60th anniversary with the paper, in 1946, he reminisced with old timers on the staff and had a quick greeting for the new ones; when he was presented with a box of golf balls his hearty shout could be heard above the cheers of the staff. The Directors, with some fear lest he be not up to it, tendered him a dinner on his 90th birthday, January 1, 1947. He had a great time, drank and smoked cigars and yarned as of old. This may have been the spur to new activity, for he accepted re-election as Chairman of the Ottawa Hydro-Electric Commission, was delegate-at-large to the Tory convention that elected George Drew leader. It was, though, an act of courage as much as of actual interest. His friends were slipping away, and he feared being an "old fogey" around the office so came there now only rarely. It was a time that reminded me of a ride back from a cemetery with him about ten years earlier. He went to a lot of funerals and towards the end would occasionally ask me to go along with him. On that day he hadn't known the deceased extremely well, but he was another one "gone." We drove in silence until he said: "Norman, let me give you a piece of advice. To the extent we can choose our friends, see to it you have a number of them younger than you are." I made brief comment of understanding and left him with his thoughts for he was upset. But no one ever needed to straighten up P.D. Ross. About six blocks from his house the kids were kicking around a football in the school yard. "Football already! I remember how I used to like to see the seasons change for always it brought a new sport. I was lucky, I liked every sport. I must see some of those games this Fall." He walked into his house, strong and tall.

What Changes He Saw
Just to see him walking was evocative of how long he had walked, and with such purposeful yet sensitive strides. What a journey over years and history and customs, from 1858 to 1947! I have a faded photo of the first page of *The Evening Journal,* Dec. 10, 1885, just twelve and a half months before Mr. Ross became its part owner. It sold at two cents. Let's see what was going on:

> In Paris Rochefort's paper *Intransigeant* charged that not only could Pasteur not prevent hydrophobia, "but it is not sure he does not communicate it to simpletons who believe they have it."
> In Regina a Member of the Northwest Council blamed the Lt. Governor for not having informed Ottawa of the half-breed rebellion.
> On Ottawa's Upper Town market square sugar was six cents a pound, cut and split black birch a dollar a cord.
> "A Rideau street man's hen roost was robbed of several fancy fowl last night. Detective Montgomery will work up the case."

War in the Bulgaria, Turkey, Serbia arena was deemed probable.

To look at it another way: when *The Journal* was born Confederation, then not 20 years old, was still shaky. The CPR was not yet open from coast to coast. The vast North-West almost uninhabited. Other than forests our resources had been hardly touched; there was little wheat, little gold, no nickel, little developed water power. Canada's outside trade was negligible, only Montreal and Toronto were known outside themselves and Ottawa was a town of 36,000—its main street, Sparks, was a quagmire much of the time and the sidewalks were of wood planking.

"The world knew little of practical use of electricity," he once recalled; "nothing of airships, motor cars or motor boats; nothing of radio, of X-rays. Street cars were drawn by horses, moving pictures remained long unheard of. Most of the steamships of that day could be carried across the Atlantic on top of many a modern steamship. The biggest and fastest newspaper press in the world could not print in an hour as many copies as *The Journal* press can print now in five minutes."

He Kept Apace

Yet even in his last 25 years P.D. kept up to the times. Principles he would stand by, but out-of-date policies and thoughts he'd chuck overboard. He was for years against public ownership, but when the need came for providing cheap electric power he championed Ontario Hydro. He would wield a tough partisan pen during a campaign and give money to candidates who had their heads on straight. But if the election was lost it was back to work in good cheer, no hurt pride, no nourishing of grudges. I suppose today he might be a bit anti-American, would feel stoutly about Canada having to stand on its own feet, but I doubt he would support extremely protective measures. He would want to be loyal to things British, but not blindly. Ross was never a little Canadian. Though he attained success and wealth, he never relaxed his principle that labor should be given a fair shake. At 80 he was interviewed by R.E. Knowles of the *Toronto Star* about the then vigorous discussion between capital and labor.

"The one thing that capitalists in this day need particularly to look to is to develop a different attitude towards others than themselves."

"Is that for publication?" asked Knowles.

"Yes, why not?"

"Capitalism must learn that human beings are more than money. Employers must learn to treat their men not only with justice but with generosity. We need to learn, and to act on it, that the under-dog is as good as we are."

I cannot imagine Ross being opposed to today's trend to better welfare. He would fight against a man being paid for doing nothing if he were able to work, he would oppose waste in welfare, but I'm sure he would declare that the world owes all of us a chance to earn a living, and a decent one.

Jan. 1, 1858—July 5, 1949

Two major operations in 1948, when he was 90, didn't much sap the extraordinary vitality of P.D. Ross. In the late Fall he played golf occasionally, with much joking but still on the fairway. He kept up his interest in *The Journal*, and in Ottawa Hydro Electric, of which he was chairman until five months before he died, having been a member nearly fifty years. In January of 1949, just after his 91st birthday, he accepted renomination as honorary president of the Ottawa Valley McGill Graduates' Society—a decision that pleased him as well as them.

About February his doctor advised him to remain home, though he still used it as a kind of office, including holding there an important Hydro-Electric meeting. But though the strength was running out, his serenity held fast. His still being honorary chairman of the Board of Governors of Carleton College (now university) adds to the poignancy of this letter he sent Carleton just six weeks before he died:

May 26, 1949

Dr. M.M. MacOdrum
President,
Carleton College,
Ottawa, Ont.

Dear Dr. MacOdrum:

I am very sorry to be unable to accede to your invitation to me to preside at the Convocation of Carleton College on May 31. I am proud of Carleton College and proud of you—but my personal activities are done.

Maybe I will be out in God's green world again—but probably not.

Meanwhile, with regard and admiration, I am

Yours sincerely,
(Sgd) P.D. Ross.

P.D. Ross died at his home at 17 Blackburn avenue at three o'clock in the morning of July 5, 1949; ninety one years, six months and five days old. His physician said: "Mr. Ross had been suffering from physical exhaustion for some months which was gradually becoming more pronounced, until finally he died of hypostatic pneumonia."

At two o'clock two days later a private service was held at his home for relatives and close personal friends. Then the mourners crossed the street to the fieldstone edifice, All Saints Anglican church, where Mr. and Mrs. Ross had worshipped since 1891.

People unable to get into the overcrowded church lined the nearby lawns and sidewalks. Everyone was there, you might say, Prime Minister King and Premier Frost and a phalanx of statesmen and public figures. There, too, were sportsmen of three generations, newspaper colleagues, men and women he had joined in almost every type of social service and charity work. Labor leaders were there, painters and poets, linotype operators and hydro men, civic leaders and representatives of the federal and provincial public services, and of health and hospital organizations.

Mr. Ross had asked that the service be brief and simple. There was an air of profound thought and respect; an era as well as a man had passed. The rector intoned, "Lord, Thou has been our refuge from one generation to another," and, a little later, he prayed that "when we quit serving our generation we may be gathered to Our Father, His work done."

As the assembly made its way down the church steps the All Saints bells rang out, "O God Our Help In Ages Past," cheerily, I seem to remember —bells the Rosses had come to feel their own. In quiet, leafy Beechwood cemetery Philip was buried alongside Mary. A great mound of flowers sang out against the grey headstone and the background of summer-green maples.

I still see the knots of people who paused to bow as his body was driven through the streets of his city. I feel, still, the emotion in the faces of some of the older *Journal* men, and others, whose sense of personal loss was greater than they had perhaps realized. I can still feel the quietness of *The Journal* operation for several days following his burial.

But those are personal thoughts. Let's note, by quick glimpses, how his community and country felt:

> Prime Minister Mackenzie King: "Foremost as a citizen not of the capital alone but of our Dominion . . . a career distinguished by kindly and generous acts and unfailing efforts to further the public good, though belonging to different political parties, often bitterly opposed, I may claim, I think, that keen as the differences were our friendship stood the test of time for half a century."
>
> E.A. Bourque, Mayor of Ottawa: "One of the finest citizens Ottawa ever had. He appreciated the duties and privileges pertaining to citizenship and he fulfilled all his obligations in this respect with courage, generosity and judgment."
>
> H.S. Southam, publisher of *The Ottawa Citizen*: "Canada loses one of its truly great sons. . . . His going leaves a void impossible to fill."
>
> Victor Sifton, publisher of the Winnipeg *Free Press* and at that time President of The Canadian Press: "He not only maintained the highest principles of journalism, but frequently established standards which were not only the admiration but also the envy of his contemporaries."

Similarly I will quote from only a few of the scores of editorials written to his honor:

> The Hamilton *Spectator*: "The man and the newspaper were inseparable: they grew up together and each was a reflection of the good qualities of the other."
>
> *Le Droit*, of Ottawa: "To no one is the word 'sterling' more applicable to describe his qualities as a man, a writer, a citizen and sportsman. Ottawa's French-speaking Canadians have been happy to recognize

that he was of that class of Anglo-Saxon in whose make-up fanaticism held no part, a great newspaperman and great English-Canadian.''

The Lethbridge *Herald*: ''No one ever had any strings on the man or his paper.''

The Montreal *Gazette*: ''For him the struggle of life was not a burden but a stimulation, something to call forth and test what a man has in him.''

La Tribune, of Sherbrooke, Que.: ''The fragrance of printed matter was sweet to him and was in no way staled by the sunshine of success.''

Such thoughts from outside the paper warmed all of us inside it. Yet for the record perhaps I may show what *The Journal* felt. The editorial the day after his death was headed ''P.D. Ross: Man and Editor; by his associates.'' E.N.S. first talked it over with Grattan O'Leary, Tom Lowrey, Vernon Kipp and me. Grattan wrote the greater part of it, but all had a hand in it. After the funeral we had a second editorial, ''A Man With A Great Heart.'' I guess it was born of the feeling his friend Duncan Campbell Scott had voiced years earlier in closing one of his poems: ''O take ere yet you say good-bye, the love of all the earth.'' I select just a dozen lines from the more than two columns we wrote:

Beneath the rugged exterior of P.D. Ross there was a great tenderness. Sham he hated, and wrong; but he had understanding and compassion, the gift of forgiveness. Above all, he was just. This quality of justice became the dominant creed of his life and sometimes became a haunting fear, lest by tongue or pen he had in haste inflicted hurt or wrong. He maintained his own beliefs against all the temptations of friendship or the influence of his private relations with public men. He said to his editors: condemn a man's policies as much as you like, but leave his personality alone. . . . His, in truth, was a soul of beauty, a soul of compassion and pity. He never moved in the closed circle of material satisfaction and untroubled self-approval; he was incapable of gross self-seeking or of anything that brought hurt to sensitiveness, to spiritual faith, to naked lonely thought. He practised citizenship. He was a man who was simple and kind and good, who left his community the better because he lived in it.

There spoke his paper, his colleagues, men in the newsroom, in the ad rooms, in the mechanised rooms, in the circulation trucks—all of us in *The Journal* family.

This great gentleman who strode the years and gave himself to their joys and troubles with equal caring and humor, was one of the students who took the horses out of the sleigh at the gates of McGill University on February 13, 1878, and pulled the Governor General, Lord Dufferin, up the central avenue of the campus to the steps of the Arts Building. For another 70 years he was ever straining to draw his own honest weight in the forward movement of mankind, and especially of his Canada.

E. Norman Smith

How can a son write of his father without singing big or singing small? Or without *seeming* to do one or the other? Specially if the work at hand is a recollection of three very able Canadian journalists and the father is in the middle of so renowned a pair as P.D. Ross and Grattan O'Leary.

But I was there, I saw all three build a tradition. All three made their unique and distinguished contributions. I may be biased in writing of my father's role in that tradition. I would be blind if I didn't write of it; the careers of all three were inter-dependent.

Each was a paradox. Ross was a poetry-loving adventurer with rock-like integrity in an athlete's frame. Smith, a sentimental man and a musician, was called by O'Leary a "superb" editor and exacting journalist. O'Leary himself was a vivid writer, a sage disguised as a troubadour, a benign thorn in the conscience of all politicians.

This sketch of my father has something of the story of the immigrant who started at the bottom, and loved it there as well as at the top which came later. In that way it is a tribute to so many Canadians who have come up the hard way.

Quickly to Fleet Street

My father was born February 3, 1871, in the bustling city of Manchester, England, which perhaps accounted for his ardor for the beauty and quiet of the countryside—any countryside. His father, John Walker Smith, was a Yorkshireman born in Scarborough in 1835, two years before Queen Victoria came to the throne. His grandfather, also a Yorkshireman, had trained with the militia on Scarborough beaches to repel the threatened invasion by Napoleon. His mother, Anne Bourne, was born at Battle, the scene of the famous battle of Hastings in which King Harold was slain. But when Dad settled in Canada in 1894 he scarcely looked back. His accent clung to him, mildly, but his sentiment, his politics and his general outlook became wholly Canadian. When I came home after working for several years in England he joshed me, not always lightly, for having gone overboard for the British.

Dad's father, a foreign lace buyer for a Manchester wholesale house, told of going into Paris on one of the first food trains after the lifting of the German siege in 1871. About five years later he went into business for himself as a draper, first in Manchester, then in Reading and finally in Croydon:

> I got my education, such as it was, at the "British School" in Croydon, and at 16, and for two years, I was a "pupil-teacher" under the Croydon School Board. In that capacity I received a secondary education equivalent to our senior matric in Ontario. But I didn't like teaching, so I taught myself short-hand while an office boy in Fleet Street. At the same time I took a correspondence course for the Civil Service examination.

But then luck blew in the window, as he used to say. On answering a "small ad" in the paper he was taken on as a second secretary, "amanuensis they called it in those days," to Edmund Robbins (afterwards Sir Edmund), the General Manager of the Press Association. This was about the equivalent of The Canadian Press, though the P.A. concentrated on British news and Reuters collected the foreign news. Dad described this experience:

> The office in Wine Office Court, near the Cheshire Cheese in Fleet street, was a small red-brick building. They wanted a messenger who

also had short-hand. I used to take the tram from Croydon to London Bridge and then walked about a mile. All traffic and trams were horsedrawn, and when it rained you'd get covered with mud. Robbins was visited frequently by prominent newspaper editors and senior Reuters men. At 18, their talk fascinated me. How could there be men who had seen such things and could produce such news reports! One of my tasks was to write letters in ink on dampened paper which in a letterpress made carbons. But because of my shorthand they started sending me out with reporters to take down important speeches verbatim—at 120 words a minute. Salisbury, Gladstone, Morley, Chamberlain—the glamour of seeing and hearing great people got me, so I went nights to King's College in the Strand to improve my short-hand to 200 words a minute. But mind, though I became a reporter I was only "helping" to cover the great events.

There were speeches of Parnell, Labouchère, Randolph Churchill, Harcourt, Balfour. I was in on the Whitechapel "Jack-the-Ripper" murders, and the "baccarat scandal" in which Edward VII was interested. I covered Sir Charles Russell's cross-examination of Piggott on the Parnell Commission, and the Irish Party's meeting to decide the fate of Parnell.

Either in Robbins office or on a job or in the Press Club, he saw and talked with such as Bernard Shaw, Conan Doyle, Gilbert and Sullivan, Ellen Terry. "Remember, these weren't my friends, I was just a kid." His shorthand skill got him the respect of some notable solicitors who used to ask that he cover their cases—which in turn brought him news tips and some standing with the senior newsmen: W.T. Stead, T.P. O'Connor, George Augustus Sala, Moberly Bell, Massingham. He became steeped in Fleet Street tradition. He roamed knowingly about London in the footsteps of Dickens and Wren. He took every press pass or other chance to see good plays and especially to hear good music. It became touch-and-go a little later whether he would make music—the violin—his life's work. Forty five years later, when I was working with CP in Tudor Street, a huckster's call from Fleet Street, he was in London for a few days and we spent hours walking about the precincts. Here was so-and-so's office, there was where a reporter was attacked by a Member of Parliament, this was the Temple Church where he sneaked in as a choir boy uninvited (but was asked back); that's where the horse tram dropped him, up there was where he sat in the big trial. And, as we walked across a courtyard—"If I am not mistaken, my boy, when we turn the corner here into that passageway there's a large window with a deep sill on the sidewalk side where I used to bring my sandwich at lunch time and sit in the sun, out of the wind. . . ."—and there it was.

There was little money around my father's Croydon home, but a lot of easy "wholesome" happiness. His mother and father were not great readers but they encouraged him to read everything he could get his hands on. Older reporters were glad to feed his interest by loaning him books. His mother wrapped them carefully for him to return: "I think perhaps she knew it might encourage them to lend me more." But music was foremost in the house, the airs of the great religious masses, of operas, operettas, hymns ancient and modern. Before long Dad became more than proficient on the violin and he and his sister played duets. "We practised in the early morning, and evenings, on arrangements of Bach, Mozart, Handel, and had tremendous fun. We would wind up a sonata with great flourish and sometimes cheer ourselves as though we were the audience, laughing and crying at the same time. Besides, we were pretty good. We would spend what change we had for seats up in the gods at the great concerts, and we'd go about to whatever churches of whatever denominations were 'staging' a Messiah or some special work."

Young Man Went West
The freak of short-hand skill, as he put it, set his ambitions high. He must have kept a level head, however; for after being with the Press Association four years he decided, "I had started too high." He wanted to get into news-writing and editing, and to do that he had to be a reporter, not just a short-hand man. Besides, he thought he should take a look around a bit before anchoring in Fleet Street. There had been offers from the Calcutta *Englishman* and the Singapore *Straits Times*, for a junior reporter. "But my father said 'don't go East, go West.' " So when in 1893 an offer came to go as correspondent of the National Press Agency to the Chicago World's Fair (two months, all expenses paid) he jumped at it. The PA manager told him he could have his job back if he returned, but it seems neither of them expected that. He landed at New York in April of 1893, believing it a good

sign that the tallest skyscraper was the New York *Times*. He saw President Cleveland open the Fair, the first of the "electric" exhibitions, but I don't recall his telling me any more about the Fair, or about Chicago, except that for a man without friends and money, it was a "terrible place." But he was damned if he was going home right away. There was a challenge to the bigness of this continent. "Besides, there was good music in Chicago, and I was able to pick up side money with my violin in small and large orchestras." After his work with the Fair, he went to a paper called the *Chicago Inter-Ocean*, mixing with "a sharp bunch of reporters who could drink pretty well." He then edited a couple of small trade papers for nearly a year—The *International Confectioner* and The *Caterers' Journal*. I have a sheet of the stationery of the latter, resplendent with its emblem. Either the *Confectioner* or the *Caterer*—or someone, for he was also doing special correspondence for British papers—sent him in 1894 to Woodstock, Ontario, to cover a livestock fair. This has ever since tickled his family. We figured he knew a horse from a cow only because cows hadn't hauled the London trams. But something happened in Woodstock. "I saw the Union Jack flying over the fairgrounds, and knew I wanted to come back to it." On a side trip to Hamilton that same year to meet his Uncle C.R. Smith, Secretary of the Hamilton Board of Trade, he met Bessie Sarah Irving, of nearby Dundas, and in March 1895 they were married. My mother had been born in Dundas in 1868, her father being William Bell Irving and her mother Sarah Weaver—of Scots and Dutch descent.

Through the Toronto Mill

In the summer of 1894 on one of his subsequent visits to Hamilton he went over to Toronto to "look around." He was hired as a reporter by Walter J. Wilkinson, then news editor of the Toronto *World*. Hector Charlesworth was also a reporter there at that time and they became great friends. Other reporters in Toronto whom he came to know well were Joe Atkinson who became owner of the Toronto *Star*, Stewart Lyon who became editor of the Toronto *Globe*, and "Bert" J.H. Woods, who became publisher of the Calgary *Herald*. By the Spring of the following year E.N.S. (as I'll call him now) was named to go to Ottawa as sessional correspondent for the *World*, and his marriage was pushed ahead to facilitate their moving to Ottawa. But just before he was to move the Tory Toronto *Empire*, started by Sir John A.

Macdonald, was amalgamated with the *Mail*. This freed Fred Cook, experienced Ottawa correspondent, to become the *World*'s man there, and Smith lost out:

W.F. Maclean then fired me in one of his fits of economy —Charlesworth and I were the highest paid reporters at $15 per week. I was left jobless with a new wife in a strange country. It was the only time in my career that I was fired. Two days after receiving my "notice," luck blew in the window again. I learned that Andrew Pattullo was in town. He was owner of the Woodstock *Sentinel Review* and a member of the Ontario Legislature. He was leaving on the five o'clock train, so I got on the train with him to continue our talk and by the time we got to Mimico I was to be what he called his "practical editor." It turned out a break of fortune, for I was able to acquire some knowledge of Canadian life in a smaller community. In that three years, incidentally, I became Secretary of the Oxford Cheese Board and organist of the new Knox Presbyterian Church—the church I recall cost $46,000 and the organ $3,500, a lot of money then. I also got mixed up in the political campaigns with Pattullo and James Sutherland, including the Laurier victory in 1896. I remember after one of the big election meetings some enthusiasts let off huge firecrackers in our office and ran through the composing room and pied all the type. James Sutherland afterwards was in the Laurier Cabinet.

As we talked that day, I asked how the switch from violin to organ had come about. In London and in Chicago, he said, he had played the violin, but in Chicago he realized that to go further with it would require all of his heart and time, and his commitment to journalism was the greater:

I put away my violin and did not play it again—a question of vanity, partly,—it hurts to play badly for want of practice. Besides, the piano or organ you can play for the happiness of others as well as yourself. I had always played the piano and done a little at the organ so the change was not so difficult. The team play required between organist, choir and congregation in a church was rewarding; and later on in Toronto, though I didn't take any full time work as organist, I did "relief" in many churches including the large Metropolitan Church which I can still feel up and down my spine.

When I was working with CP in Toronto in the early thirties we would get together for a few hours on one of his business trips there and go for walks. In that church he had played for a wedding service and at the reception after "most of us" got rather drunk; in another church the organist had July off and his little organ box was like an inferno, in that hall [Massey Hall?] he was invited to try to sing one of the minor roles in a Handel work and didn't survive—"I was all feeling and no voice."

In 1898 Walter Wilkinson, who had hired him to the *World* in 1894, was Managing News Editor of the Toronto *Mail and Empire*. Wilkinson offered him the post of telegraph editor, a congenial prospect, for his friend "Bert" Woods was then City Editor and he himself knew a lot of the Toronto press people. It was quite a brisk period for telegraph news: The Spanish-American War, the Boer War, the death of Queen Victoria, and the general yeasty effect of the turning of a century at home and abroad. After a couple of years, when Woods left to become head of a publishing business, E.N.S. was made City Editor. "A great time was had by all, for with such men as Hector Charlesworth, J.A. McNeil (who became Managing Editor of the Montreal *Gazette*) and J.V. McAree, one of the best reporters and essayists in the business, we had a good news report."

But all that desk work in Woodstock and Toronto was making E.N.S. want to get out among people and write. In 1904 the Rev. J.A. Macdonald, the "pictureseque" editor of the Toronto *Globe,* offered him a job as special writer. He soon found himself in Newfoundland investigating the feeling of that colony toward entering Confederation. There weren't any such feelings then, he reported—45 years before Joey Smallwood pulled it ashore.

A spell in Ottawa followed, in the Parliamentary Press Gallery. Then a tour of the United States to inquire into labor conditions, and an election tour with Laurier. But the career of the roving writer was cut short, for the *Globe* wanted him to take the higher post of City Editor. It may have disappointed him, though he wrote later of the valuable experience he then gained with Mr. Macdonald and Stewart Lyon, the active editorial executive.

He Buys an Ottawa Paper

At the end of November, 1905, his friend Bert Woods told him he had just had an offer to take over the *Ottawa Free Press*, and added: "I can't, would you?" "I'll take on anything that has prospects," was the reply. On Friday, Dec. 2, 1905, a telegram invited him to go to Ottawa immediately to consider an appointment as Editor and Managing Director of the *Ottawa Free Press*. He took the train that night and met P.D. Ross next morning. By Saturday noon he was offered the position, a condition being he must assume charge on Monday of the property, which had just changed hands. He returned to Toronto on the night train, secured his release from the *Globe* and came back to Ottawa Sunday night, assuming charge Monday morning. "My salary was to be $2,500 rising in three years to $5,000. It seemed to me fabulous—my best total income up to that time had been about $35 per week. Had I known then what I knew three months later I might never have accepted! Though long established, the paper was terribly run down. Its reputation was bad, its paid circulation ridiculously small."

Who were the "owners" who hired him? There were five newspapers in Ottawa in 1905: the *Morning Citizen* and the *Evening Citizen*, the *Evening Journal*, the *Evening Free Press*, and the French paper *Le Temps*, also evening. In a city whose population was 65,120 that was a lot, probably too many for all to do a good job and survive. Indeed, the *Free Press* was foundering. It had been started by C.W. Mitchell in 1866, as a Liberal paper. By 1904 its owners had had enough and looked around quietly for a buyer. In his excellent and authoritative book *News and the Southams*, Charles Bruce looked into this transaction and concluded, as I do, that rather than see someone else buy the *Free Press* and revive it, the Southams and P.D. Ross bought it, thinking to let it simmer on the back burner. They brought in E.N.S. to look after it. It seems, however, they grew embarrassed at criticism of their owning their only English opposition (and a Liberal paper when they were Conservative!), so within a year of his arrival they sold a majority interest in it to E.N.S. to be paid for out of, and if and when, any profits accrued. To quote Charles Bruce, "Whether or not the Southams and Ross realized it, nothing from their point of view was really solved. If the old paper failed, political money would raise a new one. If it succeeded, it would eat further into the possibilities of the Ottawa newspaper field. As it happened, Norman Smith produced a competitive paper."

Fresh breezes blew in the windows of the tired old *Free Press*. I had many talks with E.N.S. about this, sometimes with pencil in hand. He used always to speak of his fortune in getting William Findlay as circulation manager, ''a young fellow of tremendous enthusiasm and vitality.'' Findlay had worked on Toronto and Windsor papers and had his own printing shop in Windsor. He was a nephew of the Andrew Pattullo whose Woodstock paper Dad had edited, and a cousin of T.D. Pattullo who became Premier of British Columbia. Before long Findlay was enabled to buy a share in ownership. As Business and Advertising Manager, he gave to Dad the aid and experience he knew he needed:

> I think we made a good team, but we had fine men about us. . . . I think of Ross Munro, a superb Managing Editor, Mike Powell, a massive mechanical superintendent and smiling comfort in trouble; young Tommy Lowrey, reporter and then City Editor who became our great Managing Editor on *The Journal* and my knowing right hand; Malcolm Brice, a sports editor with flair; Baz O'Meara, reporter who became sports editor in *The Journal*; reporters J.O. Beaudry and Chester Frowde; Joe Phillips the ad manager, Bob Smith, Frank Shore, Norman Allen and Frank Brown in composing.
>
> Oh, I tell you they made a great team, and I'm sure I'm forgetting someone. Every one of those came over to senior positions in *The Journal*. I was lucky in those early friends.

. . . And Brings It To Life

Perhaps the awakening atmosphere of the city itself lifted their spirits. The disastrous fire that five years earlier had started in Hull and swept across the West end of Ottawa had brought improvements. Lumber piles that had proved such a menace in the fire had been legislated out of the city, the site of some of the largest between Elgin Street and the Canal being turned to home-building. The Ottawa Improvement Commission, initiated by Sir Wilfrid Laurier, was beginning the kind of work carried on by its successors the Federal District Commission and the National Capital Commission. The main streets were now paved, but the residential streets in rain were still quagmires. Visitors from Britain or the States, or even from Toronto and Montreal, scoffed at the capital—but something was in the air.

In 1907, his first year of ownership, the *Free Press* did a bit of "city improvement" of its own. The paper had for years been published from a building on Elgin Street between the old Russell House hotel and the Russell Theatre. The mix of high hostelry and culture was all very well, but it was a bit heady for daily work. They bought three small red-brick houses on Sparks street just West of Bank, altered their interior, put on a new front, built a four-storey reinforced concrete building in the rear to carry the presses and machinery. E.N.S. recalled:

> It was, I think, the second reinforced concrete building erected in Ottawa. We had to bring in a Montreal contractor to put it up. The excitement of a new building helped us and we convinced merchants and readers that we were on the go.

The *Free Press* was a crusading supporter in a much larger real estate operation. Sir Wilfrid Laurier had persuaded the Grand Trunk Railway to erect a first-class hotel which Ottawa very much needed, the Château Laurier. Laurier proposed to sell the company the space at the South end of Major's Hill Park for $100,000 and to spend that money in the beautification of Nepean Point, which up to then had been more or less a fenced-in dump. There was an "astonishing" amount of opposition from old-timers, who felt it was killing park area, even though the developing of the Nepean point area would be greater than the space lost. The *Free Press* gave strenuous support to Laurier's scheme. The community got not only the new hotel, but the Central Station that today serves as Canada's Conference Centre deluxe for federal-provincial and international gatherings, and much else.

A hotel of a different color figured in *Free Press* lore. There came a letter from a commercial traveller, complaining that the hotels in Renfrew were concerned only with the sale of liquor; that their premises were crowded nightly with drunks, and that the whole half dozen or so were not hotels but dirty saloons. E.N.S. recalled:

> We printed the letter and received an indignant communication from a law firm representing the liquor men's association of the county threatening us with libel unless we retracted and apologized. That same afternoon our news editor, Andrew Miller, and I went up by train to

Renfrew. We found the hotels fully justified everything the traveller had written. Next day we wrote a terrific exposure. As a result, the Police of Renfrew brought action against certain hotel keepers and summoned Miller and me as witnesses! Hanna, the Provincial Secretary who under the licence system was doing good work in making licencees "keep hotel," provided us with a lawyer. The case was tried before a big crowd. The defence, led by a lawyer who afterwards became provincial Treasurer, was founded on technicalities—for instance, Miller and I were asked if we could prove the liquid stuff served in a tumbler to a drunken man was actually beer—and the charges against the hotel men were dismissed. However, shortly afterwards the licenses of all the offenders were cancelled and a movement was started that gave Renfrew some of the best small town hotels in the province.

They had their fun locally, too. Findlay became a lively alderman, his eyes into everything. E.N.S. never sought elective office but found ample other outlets for civic energy, as we shall see. In 1913 when he was put on the Board of Health he and Dr. D.M. Robertson had a go at reviving that department:

> We stopped "mixed" cases—of which there had been many—in the Isolation Hospital; condemned a number of shacks as unfit for habitation, banished all outside privies and wells, and cleaned up the sanitation in dirty hotels. We did enough to get us both put off the Board at the end of two years! I remember, too, that in 1907 the *Free Press* undertook to put some life into the Central Canada Fair (in Ottawa) as it was too "small-town." I was promptly elected a director of the Fair! We had to guard against going onto too many organizations for it robbed us of our newspaper time, and might interfere or seem to interfere with our editorial independence.

Hot Off the Ice

A cheerier recollection was one on sports, for the community has always been a great sports place:

> The Free Press had a fine Sports Editor, Malcolm Brice, who was

eagerly read. One night when watching a hockey match in Dey's Arena near the Laurier Avenue Bridge, with six or seven thousand people present, I thought what a good stunt it would be to have the *Free Press* selling on the streets as the people were going home an edition containing an extended report of the match, together with the result. I broached the idea to Findlay and Brice the next day and they were all for a trial.

At the rink Brice dictated a running report to Findlay at a typewriter. The sheets were passed to a telegraph operator alongside them. The report was received by another operator in the Composing Room of the Free Press on Sparks Street and set up. When the game neared its close the text was shortened, and at three minutes to play the forms were closed, stereotyped and put on the press. When the final result came it was stamped on the plate. The first time we tried this stunt we had papers selling three blocks from the arena when the crowd came out. The edition contained a several-column report. We improved on that later with two telegraph operators and a second reporter writing notes. We used to sell five or six thousand papers at eleven o'clock at night at five cents each, instead of the regular price of a cent. On the first occasion we printed pink dodgers which we had distributed to the people as they entered the arena. They told what we proposed to try to do and ended with "Watch us fall down!" The achievement was of course much more striking in those days than it would be now, with the great development in telegraph and other facilities.

He sought to brighten the paper in other ways too, particularly in broadening its coverage from city to national and international news. Perhaps London had given him a taste for exuberant journalism. The *Free Press* put out frequent "extras" on such breaks as the San Francisco earthquake, and Winston Churchill's famous battle with anarchists in a London building. A juicy murder trial the *Free Press* covered with relish, and it gave daily exposure to a flock of usurers—subsequently prosecuted and convicted —who for years had been preying on civil servants.

In the *Free Press*, of course, and in *The Journal* right up to the end of the Second World War, E.N.S. used to take a personal hand in the editing and captioning of big stories. A succession of his sub-editors told of his speed in assembly of a variety of "angles" into a main lead and putting headings and headlines on it of short sharp words. Hanging even now in the hall of the editorial rooms are framed clippings of page-one headlines run by the *Free Press* and *The Journal* in the two wars. One in huge red block letters, four inches high, was "Hell's Let Loose." He ordered it in on July 29, 1914, provoked by several days of complacency in Ottawa in the face of the coming outbreak of war on Aug. 4. The head and the paper were criticised in pulpits and elsewhere, but "We were vindicated, unfortunately." One he wrote after the end of that war has a nice touch: "Beatty's Signal: The German Flag Is To Be Hauled Down At 3:57 And Is Not To Be Hoisted Again Without Permission." He did not lose his cunning in flare writing, as we see from this sequence of front page proclamations from May 1 through May 7 of 1945, as the European phase of World War II came to an end: "Hitler's Dead—Official;" "Surrender Begins;" "Surrender Spreads;" "Huns Folding Up Fast;" "Norway Next and Soon;" "Surrender Complete."

The *Free Press* had been a Liberal paper and under E.N.S. it remained so. He was death on slanted news, however; and his editorials frequently opposed the Liberal line. He enjoyed a personal friendship with Laurier which embraced many long off-the-record talks on the state of the party and nation. He said of this friendship once:

> I remember one time George Graham, one of his Ministers, came to me for information about Laurier's views. I suggested he get them direct. His answer was "He doesn't tell us a lot of things."

A curious situation arose in Ottawa's press amid the reciprocity issue.

> When W.S. Fielding and William Paterson (Liberals) came back from Washington with the reciprocity pact in the Spring of 1911, the Conservative *Citizen* and the Independent-Conservative *Journal* strongly favored it, while the Liberal *Free Press* was opposed, "unless the British Preferential Tariff is materially increased at the same time." As the fight progressed the *Free Press* got a half promise from Fielding that the British preference would be increased. The arguments the *Free Press* had used against the pact the day after Fielding's speech, which I had heard in the House, were the arguments used later to defeat Laurier.

Another instance of the *Free Press* going against the Party, an event which caused a local sensation, was when a prominent local gentleman sought the Liberal nomination for a by-election in Ottawa. The *Free Press* went to the Liberal Association the morning before the nomination and said if this man were nominated the paper would oppose him in the by-election. The reply was that he was sure of nomination, and nothing could be done. The *Free Press* that afternoon printed a little editorial on page one indicating that if this man were nominated it would oppose him for reasons it would state later. The man was nominated by a large majority, and *The Journal* and *Citizen* and others scoffed that The *Free Press*'s big stick had failed. Several mornings later the word leaked out that Sir Wilfrid, on learning the background, had called off the candidate and would himself contest the seat. He did, and for some time held two seats in the House!

Another Man's View of It

A more impartial view of the *Free Press* is available from Harry J. Walker, an official historian of Ottawa and the Ottawa Valley. He was a newspaperman in his earlier days, but never with the *Free Press*. On June 4, 1959, he broadcast this talk about the *Free Press* over the C.B.C. Ottawa station:

> This week they are committing mayhem on the old *Free Press* Building on Sparks street. Many older Ottawa citizens will view with a twinge of nostalgia its demolition to make way for a parking lot. For the *Free Press* Building was the last survivor of Ottawa's most historic corner at Bank and Sparks streets. Its contemporaries have all succumbed to the toll of the years.
>
> Next door was the Cadillac Bar, which boasted the largest flagon of beer for a nickel in Canada. On the present Royal Bank corner was the "Bucket of Blood" saloon with its beer garden under the trees on the site of the Metropolitan Building. On the Dominion Bank corner, Rochester's Drug store sported the first soda fountain in Ottawa. Across the street was the Two Macs men's clothing emporium. On the Regent Theatre corner, Ketchum and Company were selling the first automobiles. The *Free Press* city room looked out on the Dominion theatre where such famous vaudevillians as Fred Allen, Fibber McGee,

and Mae West played the boards twice daily. Here too, de Wolfe Hopper recited his famous classic "Casey at the Bat."

The *Free Press*—aggressive and sporty—sparked the newspaper life of the Capital. It had been taken over and revitalized about 1905 by the energetic partnership of E. Norman Smith, editor-proprietor, and Bill Findlay, business manager. Norman Smith belonged in that distinguished coterie of Canadian editors among such giants as John S. Willison, Billy McLean, Fighting Frank Oliver, "Black Jack" Robinson, P.D. Ross and John Wesley Dafoe.

Ross Munro was his managing editor. Under him were the fightingest crew that ever tracked a news beat—Donald McLeod, now heading a financial house, Herb Seamen, now among England's literati, Tom Lowrey, present managing editor of *The Journal*, Charlie Barker, hustling city editor who sometimes had to retrieve his reporters' copy from the Cadillac bar; Fred Williams, Press Gallery sleuth; Bill Garvock, Buck Buchanan, Larry Nevins, Bill Sullivan, Arthur Hanna, Vince Pask, Charlie Askwith and Basil O'Meara. Mildred Low was the discerning social editor in the young capital of debutantes and dowagers. But the *Free Press* had the first girl reporter in Canada, Fay Schram, in the days when newspaper work was considered too tough for the sheltered lives of Louisa May Alcott's *Little Women*.

Under the tutelage of Munro, his young men learned to compress their news facts into crisp copy. They became competent writers in an exacting school. In the school of Ross Munro no reporter earned a byline unless the story had exceptional merit.

For sports editor, the *Free Press* had one of the best and most colorful in Malcolm Brice. Brice introduced the electrical score board to Ottawa. Traffic on Sparks street was blocked when Brice chronicled the running story of championship games on his scoreboard.

While Brice got out his pink sporting extras, and Barker made his reporters dig exclusive front page stories, Norman Smith was producing polished and probing editorials that made the *Free Press* outstanding.

Yes, some vital Ottawa history is buried in the dust of the old *Free Press*.

By 1913 the ''new'' *Free Press* was working out a little better financially. The sale to my father of a majority interest in 1907 was replaced by a second set of papers enabling him and Findlay to purchase, by notes, the balance of *Free Press* capital stock. It had developed a fair-size job printing plant that helped things along. What profits there were after paying the interest and some capital on their debts on shares, they rigorously ploughed back into the business. By 1916 circulation had multiplied by five or six times. They had added a deck and a half (with colour) to the press, installed modern stereotyping equipment, doubled the type-setting capacity—and raised advertising rates. They seemed to have arrived.

But the *Free Press* became a ''minor'' war casualty. Costs of newsprint, labor and equipment went up. Merchants reduced advertising. ''The collapse of the Sovereign Bank where we had a line of credit, and the difficulty of getting our account transferred to another bank until the late Robert Gill (a grand fellow) of the Bank of Commerce took us in, had given us some idea of the treacherous spots that awaited concerns without adequate reserves. The other English papers in Ottawa were also feeling the pinch, but of course less so. P.D. Ross was specially pressed because of his loss (temporary) to the army of Col. R.F. Parkinson, his versatile General Manager.'' Charles Bruce records that the *Citizen* had lost money in 1913 and presumably *The Journal* too was in or near the rough. The war made things worse. According to Bruce, ''War costs finally convinced all hands there wasn't room for three.''

The Ross-Smith Partnership Begins

The *Free Press* went out of existence Dec. 31, 1916, and appeared next day as a morning edition of *The Journal* under the name *Journal-Press*. Two years later the word *Press* was dropped from that mouthful. Norman Smith at once became Vice-President and Editor of the combined papers. P.D. Ross said he was getting ''tired,'' and asked E.N.S. to assume the burdens, giving him not only his great friendship but his full power of attorney for thirty years.

The consideration given E.N.S. for reducing the field of Ottawa newspapers to more workable proportions was a one-fifth interest in *The Citizen* and a one-fifth interest in *The Journal*. ''It wasn't worth much at that time,'' wrote Harry Southam twenty years later—but it was an arrangement to

E.N.S.' liking. Ross never tired of saying in later years that the wisest thing he ever did was "getting Norman to come in with me."

Which brings us, frankly, to something which in today's enlightened attitude to monopolies or restraint of trade, may seem a little dicey. Charles Bruce in *News and the Southams* reports as follows:

> More than a simple sale of the *Free Press* was involved. In a business sense, *The Citizen* and *Journal* went into a kind of partnership to end cut-throat competition. A Wilson Southam (a co-publisher with his brother Harry of *The Citizen*) memorandum written in November 1919 records that for a brief time Southam Limited held two-fifths of *Journal* stock and Ross held two-fifths of *The Citizen*. This arrangement was ending at the time Wilson wrote his memorandum; but some of its business effects were preserved for years in a series of working agreements.

I have limited vision in all this; I was not there, and have only a few of the documents. But I do have a memo about the subsequent agreements. E.N.S. says it was true that he and Findlay together received for the *Free Press* one-fifth of the worth of *The Journal* and one-fifth of the worth of *The Citizen*. "But I knew nothing of an arrangement that *The Journal, The Citizen* and *The Free Press* properties were united for a term of five years, on a basis of *Journal* and *Citizen* holding each two-fifths value, and *The Free Press* one-fifth." I had shown him a note of Ross' written to Col. Parkinson, Dec. 14, 1916, which indicated such an arrangement might have been reached; but E.N.S. pointed out this was "evidently written at an early stage of negotiations between them," and he assumed it was not finally so arranged. Conceivably, both are right: the arrangement might have been set up and abandoned within two years, and as it was a Southam-Ross affair, E.N.S. might never have heard of it.

But E.N.S. did know of the arrangement the Southams and Ross made to curb cut-throat competition. Whether he was aware of it from the beginning is not clear. A letter from Harry Southam to E.N.S. seems to indicate otherwise. He says only that "Brother Wilson sold, with some difficulty, to P.D. Ross the O.N.S.B. setup and the O.N.S.B. agreement." The Ottawa Newspaper Subscription Bureau was created by the two sets of publishers to arrange, in effect, joint distribution services. The papers agreed not to cut circulation or advertising rates to the detriment of reasonable operation and the production of good newspapers. They went even further for a while, using the Bureau to try to stabilize the *status quo* in circulation and setting up a weird book-keeping arrangement where by payments and rebates they tried to keep revenues in some parity. This profits moderator, however, must have been mostly a nuisance. Bruce found that "In practice the split had little significance. Over fifteen years the difference amounted to less than $7,000." Even so, it was a curious operation. But perhaps it did more good than harm, not only to their pockets but to the quality of their papers and service to the community. Let's leave the matter to the summary of Charles Bruce, who was never a Southam man but a Maritimer with the integrity of a schooner mast:

> In fact each paper guarded its position warily. . . . The situation was thus a kind of armed truce with neither paper, understandably, willing to drain its moat or spike its guns despite peaceful alliance. In news-gathering the traditional rivalry persisted regardless of the nominal business truce, though a newsprint shortage or a drop in ad linage might result in deals to keep news columns within stated limits. . . . On the news side a royal visit, a tough parliamentary session, or a war would push one paper up to two or three columns a day more than the other, whose senior desk men would of course respond in kind. Over the year the memoranda that flowed back and forth at intervals between the generals were fairly aggressive, as were sometimes the news and ad tactics of the horse and foot. But while they lasted, the agreements saved both papers money that would otherwise have gone into competitive promotional effort.

In due course all agreements petered out and the two companies settled down to normal newspaper warfare.

The Canadian Press
From the Ottawa scene let's move to the development of national and international news. Even in 1910 when his *Free Press* was clamouring for his attention, E.N.S. was active in efforts to build a national news service. In

1907 Western newspapers had formed the Western Associated Press and in 1909 Maritime Publishers formed the Eastern Press Association. In Ontario and Quebec there was a tendency to regional feuding between big and small papers or other groups. National pooling of news was further blocked because the Canadian Pacific held the rights to the American and world news of the Associated Press—a fact the West in particular bitterly opposed. In 1910 the Railway Commission told the CPR it must not charge more for carrying the AP news than for other news. Before long CPR recognized it was out of its sphere in the news agency field and it surrendered AP rights in Canada to the Canadian daily newspapers.

In his book *The Canadian Press*, M.E. Nichols, himself a past president and one of the founders of CP, tells of meetings in Ottawa and elsewhere at which progress was made toward a national organization to receive and distribute AP news and transmit Canadian news. The task wasn't easy, and it took many kindred spirits to triumph over regional and other limitations. Of the 1910 meeting Nichols wrote that E. Norman Smith was "militant in his advocacy of a broadly cooperative movement." Apparently E.N.S. and his old friend Bert Woods of Calgary concocted the resolution that led to the establishment of Canadian Press Limited in 1911.

What was to become known as The Canadian Press was in a sense a child of the war. Gillis Purcell, the fabulous General Manager of CP from 1945-1969, has written that although the ambition of the founders in 1911 of Canadian Press Limited was to make it a truly national organization, until 1917 it was merely a holding company for the Canadian rights of the Associated Press. The West, the Maritimes, Quebec and Ontario did exchange news of their territories but the arrangement was loose, wasteful and cumbersome:

> Barriers to a national agency were the broad, almost unpopulated, expanses separating the news organizations. Without leased wires across these gaps there could be no united association, and the cost was prohibitive. The gaps were three: Saint John to Montreal, Toronto to Winnipeg, and Calgary to Vancouver. The insistent need for Canadian unity in the Great War fused the separated news units into one. In the national interest the government of Sir Robert Borden offered an annual grant of fifty thousand dollars, to be expended in bridging the gaps by

leased wires. The sectional news bodies immediately accepted the offer and amalgamated into the national entity now known as The Canadian Press.

The "unproductive gaps" were indeed so, making it hard for government or press to let each community know what other communities were doing (and suffering) in the war. The grant was used to meet the specific leased-wire purposes for which it was accepted. Ottawa to Winnipeg, 1296 miles, $25,922; Calgary to Vancouver, 642 miles, at $12,844; Montreal to Saint John, 482 miles, $9,632. There was some talk by Borden that the Government might defray costs of war news cables, but the publishers shied away from getting too deep into the subsidy trough.

E.H. Macklin of the Winnipeg *Free Press* had been the moving spirit behind the Western Associated Press, and then for union with the others. He was a father of The Canadian Press. E.F. Slack of the Montreal *Gazette* and another early enthusiast, became its first president in 1917. There were many good minds and spirits in its development, notably J.F.B. Livesay, its General Manager. But as this is not a history of CP perhaps it will be understood why I will write mostly of the role of E.N.S. in it.

Norman Smith was named President of The Canadian Press when Slack died on Feb. 15, 1920, and was given an extended term until May 1925, to see through some pressing issues.

Early in his presidency the infant organization was rocked by a move by some wealthy Toronto publishers against the basic CP principle at that time that a paper's fee to the association should depend upon its population. But with the strong support of Macklin from the West, Pearson from Halifax, Stewart Lyon of the Toronto *Globe* and Oswald Mayrand of the Montreal *La Presse*, Smith successfully led a sharp fight against them and their supporters. He termed their requests a denial of the basic CP ideal "that the strong should help the weak," asking, "Let us look at this from a national point of view." The association also survived during his presidency a brief telegraphers' strike that had threatened to still the whole enterprise. There was, of course, the succession of problems inevitable to establishing a national news service amid war and post-war changes. But on top of that there was the decision, in 1924, to accept the suggested cancellation of the Government's subsidy and to maintain the leased wires that grant had paid for. E.N.S. declared:

> The thing was wrong and we knew it to be. There was reason for it at the beginning, in 1917, but for some years now it has been a bugbear. In The Canadian Press there is a general feeling of relief. I should like to add my personal opinion, supported I believe by members, that this cooperative, non-profit-making institution should never again accept assistance from this or any other government.

But before that and after, the main drive was to build the service. E.N.S. had immense faith in Mr. Livesay's handling of management problems, and as to financial problems he knew they would always be around but could be lived with. His own task lay, he thought, in encouraging the members to acquire a possessive pride in their cooperative. He encouraged cut-and-thrust debate as "an indication of very serious interest" bound to strengthen the organization.

As an old reporter, though, he joined Livesay in striving to improve wages, equipment and—consequently—the news report. They both sought to build an *esprit de corps* and Livesay hunted for men that would do just that. By 1921 E.N.S. said in his annual report: "All our units are appreciating more and more that our duty does not end with the distribution of a certain amount of news each day, that when we have satisfied the curious and the excitable and the morbid there still remains the most important task of all, the supplying of the accurate and carefully compiled information, domestic and foreign, that is of vital importance to public opinion." In 1922 he noted the news editors of each paper were realizing that they depended on each other, and were getting their "blacks" out to CP much more quickly. The coverage of the recent general election had revealed the staff to be drilled in non-partisanship and its reports had been printed "without hesitation by newspapers of all sorts of political stripe; no general election was ever covered so thoroughly or fairly. By the political leaders of all parties the name 'The Canadian Press' was given a new significance by this achievement." The next report had special praise for the coverage of the British election, and the closer cooperation with Reuters and the Press Association; and for the improved report on the Canadian Parliament. The overseas report, we will be noting, was something he had much in mind.

E.N.S. maintained until his death in 1957 his close and you might say affectionate interest in all CP affairs. He was Honorary President until 1936. Of his role in The Canadian Press, I have been given by Gil Purcell an opinion given him by C.A. "Harry" Day, Chief Accountant and then Treasurer of CP from 1922 until 1962 and counsellor to Livesay and Purcell in most CP matters during E.N.S.' association with it:

No matter how you examine the history of the true nationalization of The Canadian Press, Norman Smith is always the man in control.

Theoretically, nationalization of the three regional news associations occurred in 1917. But Norman Smith was the man who held the uneasy union together until it was cemented by a new city-population-based assessment structure in 1923. . . .

He was an Easterner, but he brought the Maritimes and the West together with the East they disliked and mistrusted. Helped by the hard times of the early '20s, he won from the few grudging big papers the admission that the good of all, and real strength, lay in loyal co-operation side by side of large and small.

The best chairman CP ever had for its members' meetings was Norman Smith. At the early meetings, some representatives of the big papers sought to tear the existing structure apart so as to maintain their domination. They were reluctant to compromise in the common good. Norman Smith had to dominate those meetings because that was the only way to get things done.

His influence on CP's talented general manager, J.F.B. Livesay, was a vital factor in the basic operation of the national news association in those worrisome early years. The big papers disliked this volatile, temperamental and fearlessly honest executive. I don't think he would have lasted any more than two years without Norman Smith's sympathy and support. And Mr. Livesay is the man of whom Norman Smith said: "I believe that Fred Livesay contributed to the national cohesion of Canada more than any one of his generation . . . He revolutionized the Canadian newspapers by enabling them to be national and non-partisan in their presentation of the news."

There were, too, formal tributes from The Canadian Press membership.

At the annual meeting, held in Vancouver June 4, 1924, the members expressed by resolution "the lively sense of obligations its membership throughout the Dominion feel toward him for his work as President during the past four years, for his courageous leadership, his vision, his devotion to the ideal of co-operative news service, and the free expenditure of his time and energy in bringing the Association through the most critical period in its history."

He had planned at that time to retire, but as times were busy and still troublesome he was asked to remain on another year. He was the only President ever to have served five years. At the 1925 annual meeting a second resolution stressed his having "striven unceasingly for . . . an enduring policy looking to the maintenance of The Canadian Press as a national organization . . . for the mutual advantage of its members and the people in every section of Canada. This ideal has been clarified and determined by the recent difficulties through which the Company has passed, and never before has its membership presented so united a front." They gave him a grandfather clock, hoping it "may long tell out to you and your family its clear and ringing message of the love and esteem of your fellow members of The Canadian Press."

The clock's chime was the Westminster, so familiar to him from the days when he walked, or took the horse-tram, from Fleet Street to Parliament.

And Then World News

We look now at a still broader horizon. Having been keen in his work for a Canadian news co-operative, E.N.S. set out to stimulate exchange of world news. M.E. Nichols devoted a whole chapter to this in his book, so I am once again able to let others talk of him. Nichols says:

> E. Norman Smith is the man who first conceived and submitted to the British newspaper world the project of an all-co-operative Empire Associated Press. How long this project was nursed in his meditations I do not know, but it broke loose in 1930 when he was a delegate to the Imperial Press Conference held in Britain. In Convocation Hall at Edinburgh University he explained how The Canadian Press came into

existence. "No other force has done as much to foster and stimulate national spirit in Canada as has The Canadian Press" (he said) "because day by day, The Canadian Press brings home to our people of one section of the country what people of other sections are saying and doing and so lays a solid foundation of sympathy and comprehension in the approach to national and section problems."

Nichols recalled that Canada at that time had the only national news co-operative in the Empire: Norman Smith urged the other Dominions first to organize as co-operatives and then, with Canada, to join the Press Association in establishing in London a pool of Empire news drawn from cooperative sources. He had hopes, too, that London's Newspaper Proprietors' Association would eventually come into the partnership and participate in the purchase of Reuters, thus setting up throughout the world a powerful super-co-operative.

On the whole, the appeal was favorably received. The British recognized it as an unselfish ideal to help the Empire. Theodore Fink, chairman of the Australian delegation, said "Nothing more important has been brought before this conference and nothing is more likely than this resolution, if properly dealt with, to establish the real spirit of our aims and objects." New Zealand's T.C. List approved the idea, but said "First of all, it is our duty to put our own houses in order and every country should perfect its own press association." From South Africa, Kingston Russel said "difficulties can be overcome in our country as successfully as in Canada. We have urgent need for a South African Press Association."

The resolution carried unanimously, but was referred to a standing committee where it didn't stand but lay still for five years. "Disappointed but not discouraged," Nichols recalls, "Norman Smith led the Canadian delegation to the next Imperial Conference, in South Africa in 1935, and revived the question in an inspiring address."

He opened that address by describing briefly how The Canadian Press had fostered the national spirit in Canada:

This has not been accomplished by disseminating opinion, for it is essentially a factual news service, unbiased and non-partisan—asking for nothing from and owing nothing to the politicians.

We venture to offer you what we have done in our limited way as a model for the Empire at large. . . In knowledge lies understanding and the better we grasp each other's problems the more equipped are we to help in their solution . . . Looking into the future is it fantastic to picture the Empire Press knit by great wireless stations, girdling the globe with British news, exchanged by British newspapers? Is it fantastic even to envisage this Empire Press working in close and economical cooperation throughout the world with The Associated Press of the United States, conducted on the same principles and free from government subsidies or influence? . . . But the impetus must come from yourselves, from the Dominions, from India and from the Crown Colonies, for until each of you has built up his own cooperative news association there can be no foundation for an Empire fabric.

And so, authorized by the directors of The Canadian Press he moved once again a resolution advancing the idea he had presented in 1930. This idea bore repeated reference only to *Empire* news because it was proposed to meetings of the Empire Press Union. But E.N.S.' view was that exchange of news should come to embrace American and French and indeed all news organizations devoted to truth and responsibility.

Mr. Nichols' report continues:

The resolution was endorsed; fresh efforts were made in Australia, South Africa and New Zealand to establish co-operatives, but in those three Dominions, and in London as well, difficulties arose. . . . What appeared to be London's lethargy may have implied nothing more than a gracious way of intimating that Canada was striving for the unattainable . . . But there was probably another reason, a more commanding one, for the tardy response . . . Reuters' carriage blocked the way. Its managing director, Sir Roderick Jones, in the nature of his business, disliked co-operatives; he looked upon them as destroyers of agencies' accounts. Able, crafty, ambitious, his muscled thumb was on the newspapers of Australia, New Zealand and South Africa; all of them were heavily dependent on Reuters news.

However, in 1941, coming finally to E.N.S.' suggestion of 1930, the

London and British provincial newspapers in partnership purchased Reuters, setting up a news cooperative agency. "The Reuters Trust" would "supply an unbiased and reliable news service to British, Dominion, Colonial, foreign and other overseas newspapers and agencies with which it has or may hereafter have contracts." By 1946, under the inspiration of Sir Keith Murdoch, proprietor of the Melbourne Herald, the papers of the Australian Associated Press and of the Associated Press of New Zealand became partners in the ownership, control and management of Reuters. C.J. (now Sir Christopher) Chancellor, General Manager of the "new" Reuters, speaking in 1953 to the Annual Dinner of The Canadian Press paid this tribute to CP and E.N.S.: "To my everlasting pride the organization which I serve has applied and extended the system of co-operative newspaper ownership, in a manner both original and unique, by carrying it across the boundaries of a single country; and it is interesting that Reuters as an Empire co-operative is the embodiment of an idea pioneered by one of your early Presidents, E. Norman Smith." By that time, too, co-operative press associations had been formed in South Africa and India.

The Spirit of CP

It was all very agreeable to E.N.S., but whenever he spoke of it he would recall those who had been in on CP from the beginning and on the spreading of the CP ideal out across the world. "Livesay *knew* we'd get there in the end." I have a letter Livesay sent to him in Cape Town on the eve of the conference. It ended, "Don't be discouraged if you don't get very far with the co-op idea. I would not be surprised if you had a success. Anyway I think it is a darned good thing to do and in time the seed will ripen." I have, too, a yellow telegram form from E.H. Macklin about the same time: "May every hour of your South Africa trip prove joyful stop keep your eye on the ball, your trust in the Lord; eschew mixed drinks and bring me back a short-necked giraffe."

It was the spirit they all had in CP in those early years and it has been kept green by Gil Purcell, wise, imaginative and resourceful; by his successor John Dauphinee who is hot for the right principles in news but also versed in the mysteries of modern telecommunications; by a keen staff laboring in a hard vineyard—and by the Members themselves who pull together to make it all possible. I say this with some knowledge and much gratitude, for I was myself President of CP 1970-72 and they were two of the most stimulating and happy years I've known.

A Roving Reporter

Well, those were busy pages of work in the *Free Press* and in the philosophy and substance of co-operative news exchange. From here on we can relax a bit and discover other facets of the man. I think something of himself came out in a series of seventeen "letters" he wrote for *The Journal* in the summer of 1926 under the heading, "A Vagabond Motor Tour of England." My mother had died in 1919 after long illness but he was extremely fortunate to marry again, in 1922, this time to Vessie Almeida Siddall, of Aulac, N.B. Her father, George O. Siddall, farmed there as a second-generation Canadian. The two put off their honeymoon owing to pressure of work, but in 1926 had a spree in the British Isles and Paris, driving a little car 5,638 miles in ten weeks. The articles bore the byline "By Venor"—meaning *Ve*ssie and *Nor*man, but Vessie always said she had written none of it but lived all of it.

He wrote in his opening line from Virginia Water, "Yes, the hedges *are* smothered with the white blossoms of hawthorn . . . Yes, these English lanes are as I in Canada had dreamed of them, just as they were years ago when I bicycled over them and speculated about the wide world abroad." It was a return of the native, but the reporter kept breaking in. As he knew his geography and history the "letters" were more than standard travelogue, but he kept them easy-going. The small scale of the country was a constant source of surprise. They found as they motored about that "by the time our engine has nicely warmed and we are settling down for a good drive, we have run completely across one map and into another."

Devonshire and Cornwall played their known havoc on the travellers—the hedges, the little churches, the inns, the sea across which was Canada. But it could rain, too, in the land the poets painted; and "as an antidote to cold bedrooms and colder sheets we have learned to appreciate the value of those long-handled bedwarming pans that decorate the walls of the inn coffee rooms."

And so—down a winding lane to Clovelly, and the patter of donkey's feet on the cobblestones and helping small boys gather periwinkles on the smooth boulders of the beach, one lad volunteering, "Yer fust boils 'em and then yer picks 'em out with a pin.'' Pleasant, he wrote, were ''the eats.'' The strawberries in clotted cream, or the stouter fare up North, and the buns, ''Oh Lord, the buns!'' ''Incidentally, if we learn later that there is a cake or a bun, or a scone or a pie, or a cream or a cheese that we have not sampled in its home town, how desperate we shall feel. Which do we prefer? Tell us first the locality you came from.''

Three days tramping the Lorna Doone country loosed the joints, then on. '' 'If you're going East all your troubles are over; if you're going west they're only just beginning,' was the satisfactory information given me at the pub. Great thing this desire for a beer around noon, because in addition to quenching thirst one learns a lot about the immediate district from the 'drawer,' male or female.''

Green fees for golf were usually 60 cents a day for the posh clubs and 36 for the rest, but they preferred to climb the hills or explore the towns. Loch Lomond? ''Probably its 'bonnie banks' were the limits of the poet's peregrinations; perhaps he lived in Glasgow, in comparison with which the banks of any loch would seem like Paradise.'' Fun was where they found it:

> We bathed in the sea from funny little machines on wheels and lounged on the sand or helped children build castles. We read a great deal and, despite their notorious reserve, made many pleasant acquaintances among the English and Scottish people. We never knew in the morning where we should spend the night, except on Bank Holiday when we wired ahead for one night. Side roads in England are not traps for the unwary but paths to unexpected charms of scenery and intimate contact with English rural life.

He wrote, too, of places where history had left its mark, where architecture of the cathedrals told stories not alone of beauty and craftsmanship but of Christianity's hard way, and he was moved by the unpleasantness of life for those living where the population explosion was already occurring.

It had been ''inspiration'' to tour among the relics and memorials of great men:

> They did their work, they made history, they created curves in the world's progress and passed on. ''This is what we did for our genera-

tion,'' they seemed to say, ''what are you doing for yours?'' Soon we shall be back in Canada—to wider spaces, to the land of opportunity. Surely we shall love it more because of what we have seen and thought here.

E.N.S. liked to write while he was away, said it kept his eyes open and anyway he didn't get enough writing around the paper. A couple of years before that trip to England he and his wife were on board a CPR Eastbound train when early one morning it was derailed near Savane, Ont. All but four of the seventeen cars were derailed, most of them were sprawled zig-zag along the track, one torn to kindling. Many people were injured, but none was killed. E.N.S. got to the next telegraph outlet and dictated 700 words, colorful but not lurid, for The Canadian Press.

Other series of pieces came from him while ''on holiday'': one was a ten-part sun and sea account of loafing in the Caribbean and West Indies. It was, I think, good ''reporting:'' how the sugar cane was harvested, how the colored boys sang in the choir, of the skill used in unloading freight from a bouncing boat, of eating flying-fish pie after seeing them caught in the air by something much like a butterfly net, of cricket on the green and a bottle of rum for sixty cents. But the ever-present problem of education, economics and politics disturbed him, and he asked a question to which we are now seeing part of the answer: ''. . . but what are the negroes going to do for a living, with the population growing larger every year?''

E.N.S. was hardly a crusader for black people, but always his sympathies lay with them and *The Journal*'s editorial policies were generally on the natives' side, in whatever country was under examination. On that trip to South Africa in 1935 I gather from others that he was quite outspoken to some of the white Dutch, German and English residents and government officials. He wrote from Africa another ''Venor'' series of eleven articles. Gold was the heart of the economy, but he noted that in the Rand gold mines over 250,000 blacks and less than 30,000 whites were engaged in blasting the stuff out. He dug out the figures that the average native salary—(inclusive of the cost of food, lodging, medical treatment) was 86 cents a day. For the whole body of European employes, excluding officials, the rate was $5.88 for underground and $4.64 for those above ground. ''The burden of South Africa is borne by the black man; the black in South Africa is one of those unfathomable problems that white people find it pleasanter to shirk than to tackle systematically.''

(I have a postscript to those thoughts. I was often spanked as a kid by my father, with damn good reason I guess; but never so severely as when he one time caught me, aged about twelve, telling lies about and being nasty to a negro workman who did chores for a number of cottagers near Aylmer, Que. Psychologists say a parent should never betray anger when disciplining children. Well, he was angrier that I had ever seen him and his message got through further, not just because it hurt but because I knew I had hurt him.)

Incidentally, he wrote in 1935 from South Africa that gold would always be in insistent demand, whether nations remained on the gold standard or got off it, specially in times of political or economic instability. As a reporter on that trip E.N.S. seems to have done all right. But I don't think he bought any then, and I know I didn't!

About Writing and Reading

"We are all reporters," he said one time when he was *Journal* president, "or we are nothing." A contemporary wrote of him: "News was his life, the handling of news, the treatment of news. A well-written story, an attractively presented page, clean and well-printed, always could arouse his admiration and thanks." No one has acclaimed him as a great writer, but if he had possibilities he might have consciously stilled them, for he fought shy of "great" writing. Get the facts, get them straight and present them clearly: that was his own way in editorial writing and what he wanted from *The Journal*.

I remember in the early thirties while working with CP in Toronto being very impressed by a long article a "name" reporter had written on a great Canadian event—not for CP. I mailed it to E.N.S., adding that it was magnificent! He wrote back in a few days:

> I'm afraid I have to say *I* think it was overwritten. That kind of writing for a few paras is well enough—but 3 cols. are a dreadful tax on reader interest. I feel the chap could have written the same article if he had not been there but knew the city layout and had a program. He strained after effect and got mired in it. He gave no clear picture—mostly daubs of

paint. In attempting to be poetic he got facts misstated. He has a good vocabulary but drowned in it. I think the typewriter is his curse—if he had to write with pencil he would have been more economical with words! To you if you are thinking of adopting his style my advice is—don't. I am returning the article and suggest you read it again from beginning to end. If it still appeals to you I may be all wrong—but my idea of fine writing is simple, smooth, musical writing setting forth the facts in good relation one to the other.

I pass on some more of his "advice to a young reporter." Some of it may seem to run against current thought, but I doubt that proves it wrong:

When you set out to write a story it will save you a lot of time if you just sit still a few moments and think about it, even if you are in a hurry! Frame at it, get its central facts in balance in your mind—then just write it. Color and light and humor or tragedy have their place—but don't let them run away with it.

You were complaining the other day about the heading the sub-editor put on your article. Heading writing is not easy—specially if the story itself doesn't really make clear what is the essential matter. D'je ever think of that? Sometimes as a convenient guide and reminder I used to write a heading for my story before doing the story; I'd keep it by me and often it would bring me back on course! But don't give your heading to the sub-editor, that's his department, and should be.

People—not all friends!—keep telling me you are writing interesting things from London (where I was with CP for several years), but don't forget to do some "good" reading at least half an hour every day —history or biography. You have developed a facility in reporting but have some way to go in quality of thinking and maturity in expression. Read, read, read—in the train to work, in the evening, any old time even if only for a few moments. You must develop the habit—and once you do you'll soon discover you can't break the habit and won't want to. When you were a boy you balked when I made you read Dickens, and I guess I tried too hard. All right, try Maugham and Delafield and Nevinson. Chesterton is provocative and often wise but also often wordy. Priestley and Hemingway and Buchan tell good tales. I came late to poetry but give yourself a chance to like it—have you over there that Oxford Book of English Verse I gave you?

Normally he did it more subtly, perhaps just a sentence in a letter: "I've been enjoying a little volume, Nelson's I think, a 'Shorter Boswell'—full of London atmosphere. These cheap pocket editions of the classics on good paper are excellent. I advise you to look over the lists and make a collection."

Enough of that, I guess. But—I did get the hang of reading, thanks to him, and cannot now imagine what life would be like without it. I hope I have in turn helped others to learn the value and joy of reading. "Helped?" He shoved—and had to, until I was nearly 30.

His Way Around the Office

Those were letters to a son, of course! But to quite an extent he took that personal interest in all the news and editorial men, though sometimes without their knowing it. He had immense respect for Tom Lowrey, who as Managing Editor was really responsible for all of the news product except the editorial page. E.N.S. didn't interfere with T.G.L.'s operation, but the two were very close and walked into each other's office not just daily but many times daily in easy friendship.

"His eye ranged the paper," Lowrey has told me, and he was always quick to send T.G.L. a note about a good story someone had done, which Tom passed on or posted on the board. "It was more than congratulation—it was personal gratitude for a fine job for the paper." A fire story, a music review, a philosophical touch in Bill Westwick's sports column, a beat reporter's initiative in exposing a wrong, a balanced account of a Council meeting—he missed little.

But he'd stand with T.G.L. when rough things had to be said. "If a good man was getting beyond himself, or too biased or touchy, I'd sometimes suggest to E.N.S. that he have a talk with him," recalled Lowrey. "He had a way of speaking very frankly but his kindness or personal interest in the man was there all the same. He was eminently fair in everything, not only with us but with readers and with people in the news. He'd be really sore if we had unjustly hurt or maligned someone, and he drilled into us that there was no point in writing a fair story if the heading got it all slanted.''

(I interject here the remark I've quoted before of Mike Pearson one day in a talk to the press borrowing this line from Mark Twain: ''First get your facts, and then you can distort them as much as you please.'' Mike then added: ''As for headlines, which, after all, are the only journalistic things that matter, they are, of course, outside your control—or, so far as I can gather, anybody else's.'')

Lowrey has told me that at the time of the amalgamation of the *Free Press* and *Journal*, E.N.S. gathered everyone together in the *Free Press* and thanked them all for the great job. ''We're going over there, now, but we are taking our drive and spirit with us,'' he said. ''And we did,'' went on T.G.L:

> Practically the whole gang of us went over and to the good positions. But you know, once we were there E.N. hardly spoke any more about the *Free Press*. He wanted no line between the groups. *The Journal* crew learned that he was a hell of a good news man. He still had a British accent which they mimicked behind his back, and one time a reporter strode in with his hat on at the jaunty angle your Dad used, and a stick he pretended was a cane, and called to the telegraph editor: ''Well, what does Lloyd George say today?'' We all laughed like hell and just then your Dad walked in—we never did know if he had heard. But everyone knew he knew his stuff and had tremendous experience. Before long Mr. Ross left nearly everything to E.N.

However, if E.N.S. was ''eminently fair,'' as T.G.L. has said, that didn't mean he would lean over backwards if his staff was unfairly attacked. One day a parliamentary reporter came down from the Hill with word that a Cabinet Minister had browbeat him because of a *Journal* editorial and had told him he'd give *The Journal* reporters no more news. E.N.S. phoned the Minister at once and in a voice loud enough to be heard by several in the outside hall told him what he could do with his news, and that if he had any complaints about editorials come in and see the editor ''and that's me.'' On another occasion an area MP had phoned Lowrey to criticise the anti-

Mackenzie King tone of its recent editorials and add an insinuation that *The Journal* had got a good rental deal from the Government and he (the MP) might "make a fight of it." E.N.S. wrote a three page letter of the facts of the rental in question, then this last paragraph: "This is a long letter. Perhaps it would have bored you less if I had said the same things in three words —less courteous but more in the language that you and I better understand." Then there was the Senator who wrote him protesting that *The Journal* had used the words "guts" and "hell" in an editorial criticising Mackenzie King. E.N.S. replied:

> The word "guts" is not pleasant and the word "hell" is apparently reserved for the use of parsons in the pulpits—but they are both expressive . . . King has at least half a dozen splendid men in his cabinet and it is just "hell" that as leader of a war cabinet he has not the "guts" to make them work as a team.

On leaving this view of E.N.S.' "way" with the staff I am aware I would have been more likely to hear the favorable anecdotes than otherwise. A man who cared as much as he did must occasionally have blown his top, perhaps unreasonably. But of three such occasions the "victim" told me this, years later. One had been sent in to see E.N.S. to be "straightened out" on the wrong of writing slanted political stories. "I made the mistake of arguing and he got up, closed the door of his little office, and turned around and gave me hell—and then a lesson in journalism that lifted my horizons. We wound up chatting about The Hill and I went away like I'd been given a raise!" Another told me E.N.S. finally had practically to fire him to persuade him he should get into another line of work—which he did, to great success and happiness. A man on the mechanical side told me after my father's death that years earlier E.N.S. "took me by the shoulders and told me what I must do to straighten the mess of debt I was in." Apparently E.N.S. arranged easy payments on a mortgage and other things and then never spoke of it again at work. "But after I paid it all off, he came by quietly to congratulate me. The wife and I will never forget that—we were at the end of our rope."

"P.D.R.—E.N.S.—M.G.O'L."
In the chapters on Ross and O'Leary there is much on the policies and

traditions the three developed as to freedom of the press, the role of news and editorials, the ''stance'' of the paper. We need not dwell on that here, but I might tell how those three and their chief colleagues worked together.

We saw earlier O'Leary's recollections of working with P.D. before E.N.S. joined them. I quote now from my tape-recorded talk with Grattan of the days after amalgamation:

P.D. never looked at the editorials after your father was there; he was a superb editor. If there was any disagreement, it was after the editorial appeared. They may have discussed things together but I never heard of the discussions. There just wasn't any office politics—and no friction. We were all three good friends but your father was the editor, absolutely, no question about it. This was his training. Any word or thought that wasn't working, your father would take out. It often used to make me damned mad, but he was right! I never quarreled with your Dad. I found after a year or two with him that the thing to do was to write the editorial first as well as you could and if you reasoned it fairly well he accepted it, even though he didn't believe in it. Often he'd say ''That's wrong,'' and we'd argue it out, but if he felt my argument was good he accepted it, sometimes under protest. You see, often I felt your Dad, having been on the Toronto *Globe*, was in fact a Liberal and his friends were Liberal; and so I used to think my editorials were a little suspect with him and he would think, ''Oh well, he is a professional Conservative.'' But I remember only one single case where there was a dispute between the three of us that we referred to each other. It was during Bennett's regime and I wrote an attack on Bennett which your Dad approved. P.D. got the editorial wherever he was, Carolina or somewhere, and flew into a hell of a rage and wrote a fierce letter to your Dad which your Dad showed me. So your Dad said ''Well, are we standing together on this?'' and I said ''Sure.'' We did. That was the end. One outburst.

I have the documents of that row. E.N.S. wrote back sharply to P.D., saying that he had discussed the editorial with Grattan and that he (E.N.S.) had entirely approved it and was wholly responsible for it. He said he had even added some adjectives of his own, and it hadn't been so much an attack on Bennett as on both parties and on Parliament—hence the heading: "The Holy Show of Parliament." Their exchanged notes included one suggestion from P.D. that editorials criticising the Tories should not appear while he was away. E.N.S. fired back a 15-paragraph letter concluding this way:

> I believe the article has added immensely to the prestige of *The Journal* created by yourself, and if you had been in Ottawa to see what was going on instead of being down in Georgia, you would have gloried in such an article appearing in *The Journal* and would probably have written it yourself—because the situation warranted it, and the editorial was in the public interest.

The letter ended with the words "submitted with much respect"—a chill but honest assertion. It also ended the row and indeed seemed almost to throw the three even closer together. It was the paper that won, and their personal comradeship. Significantly, this is the caption in E.N.S.' hand on the sealed envelope that contained these papers: "Dispute between P.D.R. and E.N.S. in 1932 concerning editorials. The only difference between them E.N.S. recollects in their whole partnership." Only one real row in 33 years! It was extraordinary that three such different men were able to get along so ideally so long. I mentioned to Grattan that I had never sensed even a little touchiness between them, let alone jealousy, and added that it was a tribute to him for he (Grattan) was in the middle. "It was a tribute to everyone" he replied,"—*The Journal* was a pretty happy paper." The Senator, then 86, smiled, wistfully.

A Certain Persian Poet
The P.D.R.—E.N.S. partnership was remarkable because of their differing natures. Each was comforted in knowing the other was "there," each had utter trust in the other, but they didn't spoil it by making too much of it. P.D. persuaded Dad to buy a cottage next to his own 85 miles up the Gatineau —but the families enjoyed the proximity by not abusing it. E.N.S. had been given P.D.'s power of attorney almost from the beginning, and was asked to "run the whole paper"—but he took great care to honor P.D.'s seniority and to see that everyone on the paper did. They'd drive out together to the Golf Club, but each would play with his own set of friends (P.D. was a great

golfer, E.N.S. was a great lover of walking around in the fresh air, let the ball go where it may). E.N.S. invariably called him "Mr. Ross" in the office but it was P.D. outside. E.N.S. had a way of getting P.D. to reminisce before his friends—for P.D. loved to tell stories and told them well. A favorite was of a joint dinner of the Senior Golfers of the United States and Canada, at which P.D. was the speaker. During that year a number of the old golfers had died and Ross quoted that line "Lo! some we loved, the loveliest and the best. . . ." When P.D. sat down this old chap came up to him and said "Ross, that was quite a line of poetry you quoted, was that your own?" "No," said P.D., "that was written by a Persian poet nearly 1,000 years ago." "The hell it was!" replied his friend, "He must have been pretty damn good. I myself don't read poetry, the only thing I get any time to read is the god-damned newspapers."

Speaking of P.D.R. and E.N.S.—and poetry—brings to mind the lines written just last year by the English poet Mary Bewley:

Friendship is a fragile thing
If too lightly valuing
Or holding it too tight
The magic will take flight.

Friendship is a fragile thing
Of infinite delight
If understood aright.

Every year E.N.S. would "have another look" at the biographical material he had prepared on Mr. Ross for "later" use as obituary. He'd close his door and spend several hours making sure that the facts were right, the balance true, the touch dignified and yet feeling. He personally saw to all the headings and cared immensely that P.D.'s own paper should do him fitting honor. O'Leary, Lowrey and Kipp had also helped greatly in the work, but the general planning was that of E.N.S.

When the death came he was shaken, and remained so for some time. He brought me from home a batch of affectionate letters from the Ross family. One, from P.D.'s brother, Major General J.G. Ross, brought him special happiness. He wrote:

P.D. often expressed to me the fine friendship and comradeship that you gave to him, and the great satisfaction of knowing that he had such a responsible and capable man as his partner through so many years. We all feel deeply grateful to you for the great affection that you displayed toward him, and also for the loyalty and co-operation of all those who were and are making the newspaper the great success it is today and in which he took so much pride.

I asked him if I might show some of the letters to a few in the office. "No, I'd rather you didn't, they say too much about me. But tell the men the General sent his thanks to all those who have been making P.D. proud of the paper."

"The Team"

That was E.N.S.' way; he was strong on the "team" idea, and enjoyed trying to find out what each man was good at and giving him every encouragement. Tom Lowrey, of course, was team captain, just as he had captained many a district league hockey team. Strong, honest, skilled, kind—and tough when he had to be. Let's look further around the place. Vernon Kipp, city editor and then associate editor, was a craftsman with an urbane style akin to E.B. White, and it gave the editorial page a human touch on a sweep of subjects as wide as all outdoors. I persuaded Jim McCook to come to us from CP, a trained reporter whose Scottish integrity and restraint with words so appealed to E.N.S. that often when Grattan or I had written something too free-wheeling, he'd ask Jim to "settle it down a little, McCook." Another loyal Scot was George Paterson, whom E.N.S. hired away from the Edinburgh *Evening News*. Through the years George moved quietly and deservedly to the top. He and E.N.S. seemed to speak each other's language in handling and heading great stories. I tried to get Bill Westwick moved to the editorial page, but E.N.S. retorted "That would be a waste of one of Canada's best sports editors, he's a really big man for us in this community." Back earlier there was another Scot, James Henry who put out the *Farm Journal*, and then Bryan White who moved from that task to many senior posts in the company and [a bachelor] left his considerable wealth to the Ottawa Boys Club. Still another Scot was Tom Johnstone, the expert and devoted advertising manager. Ed Brackenbury and Jack Whitehorne hurled themselves into Circulation over the decades. Lou

Lalonde, now President, was at first accountant and then the able and "all-round" General Manager and Vice-President and a man of broad interest in community affairs.

And, of course, there was John Grace, for years my constant friend and associate editor. At the end of 1972 when I had to retire owing to a health problem, his being there to take over eased my regret at leaving and brought to the editorial page a rich mind and younger approach. Then there were all the men in "mechanical" whom E.N.S. never forgot; and Jack Collins, a huge man with a light touch who tended the building as a captain his ship, and who was, E.N.S. once said, "one of the true gentlemen in the place." In his really working days E.N.S. knew them all, mostly by name and certainly by task. One summer day when I complained about the heat he turned abruptly and said "Go down to the basement and work with August Woolenshlager over the seething metal pots and see how you like it!" Very many more I would like to name—Freddie Rowse, Charlie Lynch, George Casey, Walter Gilhooly, Dick Jackson and Eddie MacCabe—but as I am writing of an eighty-year span, sheer numbers oblige me to touch on only those who came into the close association of "P.D.R., E.N.S. and M.G.O'L."

E.N.S. didn't use the word "employee," but referred to all as *Journal* people, staffers, or, in speeches, members of *The Journal* family. He rarely "ordered" anyone to do anything—he suggested. He never said "my" paper, even after Ross died. We were "all in it together," and that was another reason he discouraged bylines. To him bylines defeated the idea that "the paper" counted more than its stars. When he was able to buy some of Ross' shares at slightly below market he took care to let his senior staffers participate at the same rate if they wished—a practice Grattan and I carried on when any came along.

The presidency of *The Journal*, which E.N.S. assumed several months after Ross' death on July 5, 1949, was but a continuing of the responsibility he had accepted and enjoyed years earlier. In moving the appointment, O'Leary said the paper was fortunate that there was available "one who, to the full knowledge of all of us, and on Mr. Ross' oft-repeated testimony, has been for more than 30 years the spearhead of this newspaper's growth, one who has contributed to it the great assets of wisdom, of experience, of great business understanding, and above all of knowledge of what a newspaper should be about." In his reply, E.N.S., who was then 77, stressed that his carrying on would have to be a team operation if it was to flourish. "We have been proud of the traditions of *The Journal* but these have been built up gradually. They are not all cobwebs, many of them are new. Traditions are being created all the time. Let us see to it that they are good ones." O'Leary and all the rest of the team served him and his principles loyally and with all their skill for his remaining eight years. He knew it and was each day touched by it.

His Wider Life
These pages have necessarily all been about his being a journalist, but his interests were extraordinarily broad in community service. We've noted his being with the Board of Health and the Central Canada Fair—but greater work was ahead. He was a Trustee of the Collegiate Institute Board from 1926 until 1931, and as to that there is an interesting story. One who served with him told me that in his early months he wondered why the Trustees should concern themselves only with the appointment of janitors, playground maintenance and the price of fuel. The meetings usually adjourned within an hour. E.N.S. led a movement which gradually changed their nature: trustees were soon able to hear from teachers of the problems in education, and in turn to express to the professionals what might be the views of parents. In particular E.N.S. felt more should be done in secondary education for students who would not go on to university. In 1929 the Board opened a new High School of Commerce on Carling Avenue so that "students may receive instruction in commercial practice, accounting, shorthand and typewriting, and may also study the principal subjects of an academic course." I was told by one who knew: "Your father was one of the enthusiasts who got that through; those words on the plaque just inside the door were written by him."

The Ottawa Civic Hospital, however, was his most rewarding outlet other than journalism. For nearly 17 years he gave it much of his heart and concern. City Council appointed him a Trustee in 1931; he became chairman of the Board of Trustees in 1941 and was re-elected each year to that post until he resigned in December of 1947.

As in the Collegiate Board he sought to increase the usefulness of the trustees. In an address to the Board in his closing year, he recalled that at his first meeting the most exciting item of business was the opening of the sealed envelopes containing tenders for the milk supply. The price of coal, insurance and nurses' gold pins had come up at subsequent meetings, but the quality of nursing or equipment or medical attention seemed to be left entirely to the medical staff. "In practice, not even the Superintendent had a voice on the doctors' Advisory Board, nor even on the Medical Board." Both those boards were entirely elected by the doctors themselves. He recalled that some had regarded his enquiries as interference—what did a journalist know about a hospital? He decided that as he had been named a "trustee" by the City Council it was his duty to look after the interests of the people of Ottawa, who owned the hospital, and that those interests must include the administration of the hospital. He had stressed to the Board and the doctors that he was not "against" doctors, but that it was not in their interest nor the city's that the Trustees had "turned over to the doctors all the functions for which a hospital is created." Indeed, he pointed out, an Ontario High Court judge had recently ruled that an action for damages for malpractice against a hospital could not be sustained if the governors of that hospital had taken "reasonable precautions" in the appointment of its medical staff. E.N.S. had pressed for changes in practice, and before long the hospital's by-laws were replaced. Doctors were to do what they could best do, and trustees and superintendent, what they could best administer. Out of it grew a new spirit of cooperation. It was his word, "teamwork" all over again. This time the aim was to improve the heart and strength of the hospital as an institution for healing. There came letters and resolutions from doctors, nurses and city bodies, appreciating his work in guiding things onto a healthier track.

They were, of course, years of growth in all hospitals. I am not suggesting the extension of buildings and services and the doubling of patients in his time were due to his chairmanship. But he was, I think, the man for such a time. A particular "thing" of his was to give greater recognition to the role of nurses in the life, decisions and service of the hospital. He encouraged greater training, better facilities and better living conditions for the nurses. He himself provided a good deal in prizes and library furnishings, and even the playing of the piano at Christmas parties! He was greatly touched when, six years after retirement from the Board, he was asked to "turn the first sod" for the new Nursing Education Building. He was made the only "patron" the School of Nursing has ever had.

I have a personal story on this phase of his life, revealing much of himself. He was 76 when he retired from the hospital, and all the while had been a very active leader of *The Journal*. Mornings at *The Journal*, afternoons at the hospital, and phone calls about both in the evenings—the work load was concerning his colleagues, and I was asked to suggest as firmly as possible that he should retire from the hospital at the end of the year. He replied, patiently, that it was true he worked pretty hard at both, but each was a relief from the other:

> By the time I leave my *Journal* desk I am a bit tired of it, but after a beer and sandwich at home and a bit of a walk I am refreshed and interested to think about the hospital. To think about things done and not done at *The Journal* all afternoon would just bring on the health strain you seem to fear, whereas now my health is better than yours! By evening I'm relaxed and ready for a bit of piano or bridge or family talk and a good sleep. I'm lucky to have such a great combination, my boy; the paper, the hospital and the family. But, I'll give thought to what you have said.

Several months later he told the hospital he would resign at term end, but explained to me it was "not because of my health or hard work but because I think it is time the hospital benefited from a new chairman with new ideas."

The community was generous in its praise of him as he retired, but I will quote only an editorial given top position in *The Ottawa Citizen*:

> Mr. Smith has been an outstanding chairman, has not only done a job of remarkable value to the city but has made the hospital the subject of intense personal study. He has served usefully and unselfishly on the hospital's governing body and become an authority on the administration, in all its phases, of such an institution. He has taken his duties seriously and prepared himself conscientiously to give the best he has to the chairmanship. If Ottawa Civic has become one of the outstanding hospitals in the country, notable on both its professional and administrative sides, it is in no small measure due to Mr. Smith's informed and public spirited service. He has put his heart and mind into his work and the public appreciates that fact.

But the man's wider interests were not all labor; he had lots of time for sports, arts and hobbies. Let's go back a bit. Prior to 1910 the Royal Ottawa was the only golf club in the district. William Foran was then a prime mover in organizing the Rivermead Golf Club, with E.N.S. its first vice president. P.D. Ross was among its first stockholders. After some years E.N.S. joined the Royal Ottawa, but I'm told he and a small group of citizens thought there should be a public course, so more people could play. Sir Robert Borden was one of the chief sponsors. In 1923 Norman Smith was associated in the founding of the Chaudière Club, first named the Algonquin Golf and Country Club. The plan to make it a public course proved unworkable; but it was developed as an "inexpensive" club. The first president was Hon. Edgar N. Rhodes, Charles Graham was secretary, and William Foran, Treasurer.

E.N.S. gave editorial and other support to the founding of almost any type of sports or outdoor club, especially those that would be accessible to people of small means. It was a hobby of his, too, to crusade every four years or so for more and better parks, and greater preservation of outlying districts for the enjoyment of all citizens. Music and choral clubs had his interest and support, and the Ottawa Drama League and later the Canadian Repertory Theatre knew him as not only a supporter but regular attendant. I don't believe he ever lashed on a ski, but C.E. Mortureux and other pioneers in the Ottawa Ski Club could always get his (and therefore *The Journal*'s) ear in the days when a skier was regarded as something of a nut.

Speaking Personally

The next two or three pages will be personal. For the record—for the family record if you like—I want to say something of my father as he was in and to his family.

I hope that our "comradeship" in work and in life has come through in the earlier pages. Ours was something of the old fashioned father-son relationship, a reserve on both sides not because we had not love and affection, but somehow "it wouldn't do" to reveal it. I think there's much to be said for the newer ease between parents and children, though that, too, seems to have produced its own problems. But I know Dad gave my sister and me great happiness in his love for us and the broad range of interests he nurtured in us; and he did that though our mother died when Marion was 19 and I was nine. I know now that my sister gave me many of the things a mother gives to a son, a generosity not early enough appreciated and repaid, for she died at only 43.

My father's second marriage also gave him great happiness. As my new sisters Barbara and Naomi and my brother Ross came along, I was pretty much out to work and my own marriage, but I was with the new household whenever possible. We were to all measures one family—a blessing which Vessie, (my stepmother, but not so-called) did much to attain. Barbara married Archie Pennie, who became vice-chairman of the Defence Research Board; Naomi married Tony Abbott, son of Douglas Abbott, former Liberal Cabinet Minister and Justice of the Supreme Court. Tony, a lawyer, resigned as General Manager of the Retail Council of Canada in 1974 when he was elected Liberal member of Parliament for Mississauga.

My brother Ross had navy training at Royal Roads, has a B.A. from McGill, plays the piano well, has spoken French since he was about four, and makes and keeps friends without trying. He has been reporter and City Editor and Features Editor of *The Journal*, and good at all these; but having a broad perspective on life, he has not let printer's ink fill him to the ears. He and his wife Diana, a daughter of the late Mr. Justice Henry Hague Davis of the Supreme Court of Canada, have found life can embrace, as well as journalism, dog-raising, riding, boating, and trying to keep up to two daughters with prize-winning minds at school and university. To get an intimate look at my father in the bosom of his "second" family, I asked Ross to give me some quick flashbacks on his edition of life with father. He dashed it off at once, and was appalled when I said I wanted to quote it as is, for it was full of vitality. Reluctantly, but characteristically wanting to be of help, he said "Okay!"

Oh, the slow meals! "Take small bites and chew them well. Don't bolt your food." The frustration of waiting for him to finish! He'd carefully peel pieces of apple and pass them around to us kids.

Reading a Christmas Carol, editing it as he went on (I now realize), acting out all the parts. "What's today?" he'd call out, and I can still hear the cockney boy shouting back.

Sing-songs around the piano. The Christopher Robin Songs, Changing the Guard at Buckingham Palace, "and Alice," and always ending up with Christopher saying his prayers . . . getting quieter and quieter.

Being taken to the movies, and how he loved Charlie Chaplin and would laugh until out would come his big white handkerchief to mop up.

Up at 31-Mile-Lake, and travelling very very slowly in the boat so he could "feel" the silence. He liked fishing, but really just to get out in the boat. And picnics, and we'd stop off at a farm and pick corn. He liked to dive into the lake and just float (he could float vertical) and watch us do running dives. Obviously he was older than most parents, but as a boy I never noticed. We used to play a lot of catch right up until I was in late teens and he about 75. When we had Triple-A ball at Lansdowne he was a real fan.

As we grew up the sing-songs changed: duets on the piano and fairly serious singing with metronome and all that. Lots of Bach, and he loved playing hymns and got expression into them without being sloppy. I've seen a dozen singing around the piano, as good as some choirs! Barbara and Naomi went on to real choral work and are still at it.

He was always reading . . . and trying to encourage me to read, which I rarely did. He could drop off to sleep without warning, the book askew on his lap; sometimes while reading stories to us. On many other occasions we'd accidentally waken him from one of his "forty winks" but he was never cranky as I am when wakened.

Listening on radio to N.Y. Philharmonic Sunday afternoons was ritual. He used to get the programs by mail, and if it was a choral mass he'd get down his old music score and follow it.

It still amazes me that all that time ago Mum and Dad sent us kids to French pre-kindergarten and then to French schools. He could hardly say "bonjour" himself. He taught us all to drive, of course. He was a good driver himself, fairly slow; but he was so busy looking at scenery he'd make us nervous at times. He told great yarns about his first McLaughlin with the rubber horn and everyone in dustcoat and goggles and how a horse once shied up and *sat down* on the bonnet up behind Aylmer with you and Marion.

He was always first up and in a dressing gown had read the morning *Journal* and *Citizen* before breakfast, often having phoned in the gist of an editorial to the office. He liked morning papers and was disappointed when *The Journal* dropped its morning issue in 1949 and *The Citizen* in 1953. I don't remember ever seeing Dad dressed before I went to school, but he was in touch with the office every night and they had orders to call him if anything broke, no matter the hour. They did.

I remember when after some years as reporter etc. I became City Editor it was for me the phone at home was ringing all evening—and he was terribly curious as to what was going on but tried not to show it! But talk about memories, here's my greatest! When I was a sub-editor on the news desk he asked me to come into his office to discuss a story he was interested in. Along came an important-looking citizen expecting an immediate audience with "the editor." Dad looked up and said very calmly: "Excuse me please. I'm having a discussion with one of my editors. I'll let you know when I'm finished." Boy, did I feel ten storeys high! I must have been all of 25.

That's Ross, all right: lively and no frills, as always. I'm sure Barbara and Naomi feel as I do that he has "caught" Dad for us all. It is interesting that he mentions E.N.S.' liking baseball; he was also a keen hockey fan of the old Ottawa Senators. I don't recall his being aware of who was leading in British cricket or soccer or rugger. Save for a continuing interest in British politics and literature he was a complete transplant to Canadian soil. It was baseball, perhaps, that brought his death.

February 3, 1871—October 18, 1957
In early October of 1957 E.N.S. had a cough that grew more obstinate than what he always termed a "cigarette throat." After some days at home it began to look like influenza and he yielded to persuasion to spend most of the time in bed. But he was propped up against pillows reading most of the time—Trollope at one time when I called. The World Series came along (in which Milwaukee beat the Yanks); and despite the doctor's order to stay in bed, he watched TV in his study. "I'm well bundled up." In a few days, broncho-pneumonia set in, and sleep, and semi-consciousness. One afternoon by pure chance Ross and his mother and I were standing around the foot of his bed talking quietly when he came to, looked about at us and with a warm smile said: "This looks rather like an occasion!" He drowsed off in a

few moments and died the next morning, Oct. 18. It was a far easier passing than he had seen endured by his first wife and daughter.

In Christ Church Cathedral four days later, the organist, his friend Godfrey Hewitt, warmed the formal Anglican funeral service with works of Bach and Handel he knew my father loved. It seemed a touch of sun upon the gathering of newspapermen, and parliamentarians of all parties, who had come from afar to join Ottawa's official and personal tribute. And so to Beechwood Cemetery.

It is not for me to assess my father's place in journalism. But I will reproduce portions of the editorial *The Journal* published after his death—written by Grattan O'Leary, with a hand from Tom Lowrey, Vernon Kipp and Jim McCook.

E. Norman Smith as editor had one ruling passion: *responsibility*. The business of a newspaper was to print news, but its privileges and freedom demanded that it be also an instrument of service. Sensationalism, the "newspaper stunt," anything that violated canons of good taste, these were abominations. "I want *The Journal*," he would tell his editors, "I want *The Journal* to enter homes with grace, as a guest."

Yet with these rigid standards E. Norman Smith had an extraordinary degree of open-mindedness and intellectual generosity towards his colleagues. No editor could be more open to argument, more willing to listen to the case of an associate. He never tried to use others as instruments for the expression of his own ideas. His supporters might sometimes feel a lack of direction, of a "line," but they came to see that this was a compliment to, and a demand on, their own integrity. He could carry this principle so far as to accept from an associate the expression of views with which he did not himself concur. Yet no one could have been more wise in suggestion or shrewd in criticism; one could not work with him and remain immune to his influence, nor without coming to admire his unerring ear for the false note, for flatulence in writing, for the sonorous phrase which papers over vacuum in thought.

His own writing was never fine writing. He would say no more than would convey the thought, and let the argument stand without trying to decorate it with epigram or wit or scoring it with emotional undertones. It was this passion for simplicity, for the spare and simple sentence, which made him superb as an editor.

But the editorial page, though he held it to be the heart of the paper, was not his first love; his true newspaper passion was for the news, for the "big story," for a daily presentation with vividness and accuracy of the world procession. It was this that kept him to the end a working journalist, never happier than when out in the news room with his newsmen taking a hand in the presentation of some big word from the wires.

But he was publisher as well as editor: he knew about presses and type and the problems of the mechanical production, advertising and circulation departments, and of the general business of the company. His standards were exacting, a reflection of his own integrity and his constant realization that *The Journal* was far more than a business —that it was a public trust. . . .

Hard on the heels of the newspaperman was the man who loved his city and gave of his time and energy for its good. His tastes were as catholic as his interests were varied. And to all of such interests and liking he brought broad understanding, a sense of proportion, exact and lucid thought.

Thus did we at *The Journal* know and honor E. Norman Smith. Thus shall we mourn and remember him.

That editorial was written by his friends of course, by his "team." The members of his family were and remain deeply moved by it.

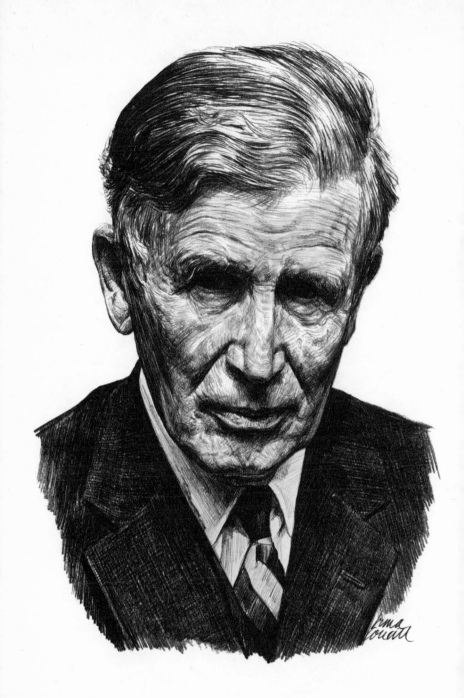

M. Grattan O'Leary

I have read the Speech from the Throne over and over again; from its first page of platitudinous inconsequences to the last page where it calls for the protection of Divine Providence—and that was about the only hopeful thing in the whole document.

That is the O'Leary the politicians feared and enjoyed. A shaft of humour in the Senate vault. He never let surroundings awe him, yet a genuine humility kept him always well this side of contempt.

Sham he could not abide. Neutrality in politicians or newspapers he elevated to head the deadly sins. He held that spirited argument was more productive than all the speeches in the world, yet he was of the best of Canadian speakers and not only honored but could quote at length the great lines of democracy's long march.

Impatient he was with the patient; patient he would be with the impatient. His religious faith was profound, of those with none his understanding was sad but kind. Old people and ways he cherished, yet in his own "old" age his companions are mostly young—friends of his children and children of his friends.

> Conservative, liberal, idealist, rebel;
> Optimist, pessimist, latter-day sprite;
> Preacher, sailor, journeyman, 'divil';
> All of their forces he called to his fight.

Raised Against the Wind

Michael Grattan O'Leary was born in the impoverished county of Gaspé in Eastern Quebec, on the shores of the Gulf of St. Lawrence where Atlantic winds blow hard. Whether or not he gloried in it then I don't know, but he has relished its hardship ever since. In a Senate discussion of poverty in 1971 he declared "I want to say to Senator Croll that I am very much afraid that, if I had been promised as a boy in Gaspé a guaranteed annual income in the future, I still would be in Gaspé in that ghetto of poverty."

Let him describe those early days, in his own words assembled by me from various sources:

> I was born in Percé, on Feb. 19, 1888. My father was born there too, his father having fled the Irish potato famine in 1847 and settled on a scrub farm area, making a life from the land and sea. I grew up in a settlement called Irishtown Road where every cabin had three pictures—the Pope, Parnell and John L. Sullivan. I left school aged eleven, but lived there until I was 15.
>
> When I was a young boy a bell summoned the workers at dawn to trawl out fish to be dried on the flakes. They were given an hour for lunch and they worked on until dusk, and often were summoned out again to work until midnight. They received, as I remember, about 75 cents a day. But the people of Gaspé also had small farms, farms which did not bring them wealth but which gave them security and a sense of manhood and dignity. They grew their own grain. They cut it with a sickle, and they threshed it with a flail. I myself engaged in those activities. They took that grain to the local miller, and brought back feed and flour for their livestock and for themselves. They killed their cattle, and took the hides to the local tannery and brought back leather, and they had that leather made into boots and shoes by the local shoemaker. They lived by the light of candles made by themselves. They sheared their sheep. They put the wool on the snowy slopes to bleach. They brought it into the homes and carded it. They spun it into yarn on old spinning wheels, and then took it to the looms, which were in most of the homes, and wove it into good homespun. While I say this

was not affluence, it was not extreme poverty, and it had the great merit of preserving the manliness, the dignity and the courage of the individual.

Now you ask me what education I had. Very little, unfortunately. But I think the present approach is wrong. Education is not something to make a man a lawyer, a doctor, an engineer or priest. It is something to make him a man. The true education is not to give a man a standard of living, but a standard of life. I speak with some feeling on this. I never went to High School but God was good to me in that I knew an old Bishop in Gaspé, Bishop Bosse. His sister lived on an adjoining farm to ours, so he sent me his books. He was a remarkable man. He sent me biography, history, poetry and novels. He once even sent me the sermons of that famous Baptist divine, de Witt Chalmers.

Upon my soul to God he gave me my life. Think of it! There was every kind of book: textbooks, novels frivolous and exciting; Shakespeare's sonnets, Matthew Arnold, Longfellow, and Yeats, of course. And Rider Haggard's "She." I never had a grammar lesson, but poetry gave me a sense of the beauty and economy of words. We had lots of Irish newspapers, from Dublin the *Freeman's Journal*, from New York the *Irish World*, from Minneapolis the *Irish Standard*. We knew more about British politics than Canadian.

We who have heard him casually talking of Parnell or Gladstone or the great British trials as though they were local politics know he wasn't romancing:

When I read these books I read them by candlelight (because we had not yet reached the kerosene stage) by candles made in our own home. What did they do for me, those books? They made me think that I must explore that outer world. I got to know about that world which is far, far beyond the Gaspé coast. It also made me know that I had to work to get to that outer world. I worked in a lumber mill at the age of twelve. I went to sea at the age of fifteen and remained three or four years. I came ashore in Saint John, New Brunswick, and worked in the Saint John Ironworks, in the Pinder nail works; and in a brewery. I worked in a hardware shop. I went up to Richibucto, a little windswept village on the Northumberland Strait and worked in a store. I got a job as a reporter in 1909 on the Saint John *Standard*, which I am sure has been a bad thing for journalism, but at least it saved my spirit and my soul. I have never thought of the state looking after me, never. I never thought of it, I expect, until I guiltily entered this Chamber in this Senate.

The man in the green eyeshade in the *Standard* office the night O'Leary walked in must have sensed O'Leary's craving for writing, for though he first said no, he added, "Well, we'll try you; go out and find a story." He did—a half column on the harbor. But the craving was only sharpened. He has told me he yearned even while at sea to get to Ottawa. It took him but a year and a half on the Saint John paper to "hear about" an opening at *The Ottawa Journal*, in 1911, and to grab the next train at his own expense.

To Ottawa and Parliament

I arrived Ottawa on the first of March at 1:00 in a hell of a snowstorm. Instead of going down to *The Journal* to see that my position was there, I wended my way up to the old Parliament Buildings and sat in the Gallery to see and hear Sir Wilfrid Laurier and Sir Robert Borden. I sat there so long that I endangered my job at *The Journal*, because I did not get back there until 5 o'clock and they thought I was not coming.

In *The Journal*'s old office on Elgin street a man he recalls as fierce-looking said: "Now look, we've promised you $17 a week, but if you don't earn it you're not going to get it." They started him at general reporting but his contemporary Arthur Ford of the London *Free Press*, recalls that "they" very soon recognized Grattan's unusual ability and transferred him to the Parliamentary Press Gallery. He is described as, "a black-haired dazzling youth, who came into the Gallery just after the Conservatives carried the country on the reciprocity issue."

It was the beginning of his long love affair with Parliament. It was to him the people's chiefest weapon, a place where men should meet as gentlemen but fight for their ideas and ideals, passionately, proudly. The bust of his head in the corridor outside the Parliament reading room may seem to scowl—but it is of anxiety for Parliament, not disdain.

Those were the days! The net public debt of Canada was about $350,000,000 which, he told the Senate in 1966, "would not pay more than one-third of the interest on the public debt at the present time." (I find that in 1972 the net public debt was $17,937,000,000 and the interest on it $1,964,000,000. Or, $89.95 per capita now against $1.66 then.) Sir Wilfrid Laurier, he went on, used to take the street car from his home to Parliament. Sir Robert Borden rode there on his bicycle. Mackenzie King used to stroll the streets by himself during the evening. "All of us who went to Parliament in those days came under the spell of Sir Wilfrid. We knew we were in the presence of a great man. He had majesty, charm and grace. He looked as if he had just stepped out of a painting."

The Titanic *Story*

For all the young man's awe was for Parliament he must have been a crackerjack general reporter. In April of 1912 he was sent to New York in a hurry to meet the *Carpathia*. The ship was bearing 705 survivors of the 2,202 passengers who had been aboard the *Titanic* when it went down in the North Atlantic on April 14. He arrived New York just hours before the *Carpathia* docked, a "green" reporter in the metropolis on one of the big stories of the age. Fifty years later in *The Journal* he recalled it this way:

The taxi got no nearer than a quarter of a mile from the dock; the approaching streets were blocked with traffic, and to make matters worse, the rainstorm had grown worse.

I quit the taxi and walked, and within minutes, which seemed like hours, I was on the right dock (I had known New York's piers fairly well when I used to go there on the *Lady Eileen* some six years before) and just in time to see the first survivors being brought down the *Carpathia*'s gangplank.

The survivors came down, some on stretchers, some by themselves, others aided by sailors. They were taken to a sort of improvised hospital in a shed, and there what seemed to me a veritable army of reporters, myself included, were permitted to talk with them.

There were no Ottawa survivors, and so my job became one of listening to the various tales of horror, and of piecing together from them the story of the *Titanic*'s tragedy.

The Journal had arranged with the CPR in Ottawa to have a wire open for me as long as I needed it, and all through the night messenger boys came and took my pages away as I finished with them. As I remember it, I wrote some 6,000 words with a pencil—typewriters were rare in those days—and finished my stint about 8 o'clock in the morning.

I think I used up all the adjectives in the dictionary.

After a few hours sleep and breakfast, I went to a Senate committee inquiry. It was, I thought, a stupid inquiry, especially as its chairman, a Senator from Michigan, a veritable landlubber, seemed to have no idea of what he was supposed to be doing.

One of the questions he asked, I remember, was whether watertight compartments were something for passengers to crawl into in the case of an emergency.

My story, which filled the whole front page of *The Journal*, and flowed over inside, had the main facts in it, I think, but it also had a lot of conjecture, perhaps too much imagination. But that, I feel, can also be said of the many, many versions of the *Titanic* story that I have read in the years since.

April 1912 was a good while ago, but last summer (1973) in his office he talked to me of his "fear" and "excitement" in such a big assignment. P.D. Ross, whom he scarcely knew and had rarely seen, rushed to Grattan's aid when *The Ottawa Citizen* took after him. "*The Journal* devoted all of its front page to my story. *The Citizen* came out with hardly any story and declared that O'Leary hadn't been on the dock with the *Carpathia*. P.D. at once announced we'd sue, and they apologized next day on the front page. Some years later I was sent to the States to investigate the best methods of filtration of water. I got an interview with the State Engineer in Boston, who said mechanical filtration was a threat to public health. *The Citizen* declared I had never had such an interview. P.D. came out with the damndest editorial on the front page 'The Libeller libels again' and threatened a libel suit again and they apologized again."

His Family
The year 1913 too brought a great event—his marriage on July 1 to Mary Honoria McKenna, daughter of Arthur McKenna and Catharine Murphy, of

Antigonish, Nova Scotia. His bride had been a gold medallist at St. Bernard's College, St. Francis Xavier University. After teaching briefly in the United States she had come to Ottawa to work in the Auditor-General's Department. Even when I came to know them 35 or more years later they seemed a young couple, the house alive with children and their friends, with fun and laughter and dogs and argument. There was always good controversy on books and politics and sport and—yes—on art and religion and humanity. In latter years Mrs. O'Leary suffered greatly from arthritis, but rarely did her smile and manner lack its old compassion and humour.

They had five children and, you might say, the seven grew up together. I recall few if any families of those 20's and 30's where the relationship between parents and children was so natural and as vigorous in its cohesive affection, though a family of seven very separate individuals. Dillon and Brian became good newspapermen in their own right, though Brian died in 1971. Dillon writes thoughtful editorials, book reviews and a cheery column on wine for *The Journal*. Owen, a Pilot Officer in the R.C.A.F. was killed in World War II. Maurice moved from the bottom to vice president, technology, in the Aluminum Company of Canada. The one daughter Moira married Frank McGee. The latter as newspaperman, public relations executive, member of parliament and grand-nephew of Thomas D'Arcy McGee, needed no spur to his Conservative persuasion. But he got it from his wife, in O'Leary-like daily dialectics, lively and loud and with the clout of a handsome woman.

The Heart of His Politics

As politics were in his home, so were they in his heart and work. As I have mentioned, I have for ten years been urging him to write his autobiography. Preoccupation with what he called "more important things" put it off. In December of 1972 he said flatly, "There will be no book, Norman." As he wasn't well then, I hesitated to argue further and set out to write this one, with his urging. Now, as he turns into 86, he tells me he is "going for the book" again—and that's great news for Canadian history, political life and literature. It is also good news for me, for I can leave to him the rises and falls of Tories and Grits, his part in the issues, tumult, grief and joy of them.

But to talk of O'Leary without touching on politics would be like discussing DeValera without mentioning Eire, or Gordie Howe without getting him into the arena. I'll not do the play-by-play of his political career, but I will try to convey the aim and conscience of it. It is too easy and careless to tab him as "the last angry Tory"—his anger and his love were for parliamentary democracy. I shall provide some of his own answers to the questions he was forever asking himself and others: where have we come from in politics and democracy, where are we going, and is that where we *should* go?

Sir Wilfrid Laurier

Three men in Canadian public life excelled all others in O'Leary's mind —Wilfrid Laurier, Robert Borden, Arthur Meighen. They made their lasting imprint on his character when he was in his twenties, and he went on to uphold their ideals for parliamentary democracy when cynicism and apathy tended to make any idealism old hat. O'Leary distilled his feelings for Laurier in an address Nov. 1, 1973, on the occasion of the changing of the name of the University of Waterloo to Wilfrid Laurier University. It tells much of Laurier—and reveals much of O'Leary as a young man:

> The snows of sixty-three winters have melted from Parliament Hill since, as a very young man, I first went there as a member of the Parliamentary Press Gallery. Dr. Johnson said of Burke that if you took refuge with him in a doorway from a shower of rain, you would know you were in the presence of a great man. That could be said of Laurier. He had a majestic presence, looked as if he had stepped out of some famous oil painting, and he was, of course, one of the great orators of his time.

As O'Leary had covered Lloyd George in a British election, had often heard Churchill and Roosevelt "and the great Irish-American orator, Bourke Cockran," he felt he could say with deliberation that Laurier at his best became "neighbor to the sun and was an arrow's flight beyond them all." He went on to tell of one of Laurier's speeches he would never forget:

> The Conservative government of the day were trying desperately to put through a bill on closure, and when Laurier rose to speak, a

Conservative member, a Mr. Northrup, sprang to his feet and moved that the member for Saint John, Sir Douglas Hazen, "be now heard." This is what is known as "the previous question" which must be accepted; enough for me to say that it prevented Sir Wilfrid from speaking at that time.

Laurier, of course, had the right to speak later, but that their revered old chieftain should be denied the floor *at any time under any circumstances*, infuriated the Liberals.

When the house returned at 8 o'clock, Laurier took the floor, the galleries crowded, the atmosphere electric. In memory I can see him now, pointing his finger at Sir Robert Borden and beginning with passion:

> The poisoned chalice you have placed to my lips today will be returned a hundredfold to yours in days to come.

Samuel Butler wrote of Bacon that "men feared he would make an end." That could have been written of Laurier that night. A silent house, enchanted, mesmerized or awed, watched and listened to an incomparable orator, hoping he would not make an end. And when Laurier, exhausted by his own vehemence, sank back into his seat, the ranks of Tuscany could scarce forbear to cheer. And the Liberals, with an intoxication of triumph, stood upon their desks, threw Hansards and bluebooks into the air, and continued in demonstration for nearly a quarter of an hour.

Never before had I witnessed such an example of the power of words to stir the passions of men.

O'Leary continued:

There was a day when, all of Ottawa in a state of excitement over a report that he was about to resign his Liberal leadership, I had the privilege of a brief interview with him. It was during those stirring war days of the formation of Union Government, when Laurier tragically found his longtime friends and captains deserting him, and there could hardly be doubt that he was thinking of calling it a day. Yet when I was admitted to his room, I found the old man reclining on a couch, reading a Life of the Empress of China.

When I asked about his reported intention to resign, his reply was characteristic. "Young man," he said, "as an old journalist, I understand your question. You are doing your job. But if or when I have to answer your question, *the answer must be to my party.*"

He understood the press, but while he was always courteous and kindly, he never gave interviews, never gave that abominable thing which we now know as a press conference, and refused to go between quotation marks. If he had a statement to make, or a policy to announce, the place for it was parliament.

Laurier was not, as I remember him, what we now call an "intellectual." But he had a thorough sense of literature, was familiar with history, could quote Mazinni, Cavour or Garibaldi (he sympathized with their aspirations for a united Italy), or quote Thiers, of France, and the names of British Liberal heroes, Fox, Bright, Gladstone and O'Connell, were forever on his lips.

Mr. Pearson, in the second volume of his memoirs, confesses that he was never a House of Commons man, that he felt uncomfortable there.

It was different with Laurier.

For him, the House of Commons was a theatre; a theatre on whose stage he was the leading actor—the star.

The objects and amusements which other men sought in a thousand ways were for him all concentrated there.

It was his mistress; his ambition; his library, his creed.

On a dull day, he would study a dictionary—a book which he pillaged to bring words to his command.

Or he would wander over to the reading room to study newspapers from all parts of the country.

I had the good fortune to hear him make the last two speeches before his death.

One was in St. Patrick's hall in Ottawa, with Lady Laurier, growing blind, sitting in the front row of his audience, and pounding the floor with her cane to lead in the applause.

The other was in London, Ontario, where he gave what he called his "last will and testament to the young Liberals of Ontario," which was this:

> Many problems rise before you: Problems of race division, problems of creed differences, problems of economic conflict, problems of national duty and national aspiration. Let me tell you that for the solution of these problems you have a safe guide, an unfailing light if you remember that faith is better than doubt and love is better than hate.
> Banish doubt and hate from your life. Let your souls be ever open to the promptings of faith and the gentle influence of brotherly love. Be adamant against the haughty, be gentle and kind to the weak. Let your aim and purpose, in good report or ill, in victory or defeat, be so to live, so to strive, so to serve as to do your part to raise ever higher the standard of life and of living.

If I had my way, I would have those words inscribed over the portals of every schoolhouse in this country.

A few months later, Laurier was dead. O'Leary was among the mourners at his graveside set in a secluded spot of Notre Dame cemetery, then in a suburb of Ottawa. Only a few stood and waited as the procession came forward. The tone of O'Leary's news story was hushed and intimate: ". . . He returned to the soil of the land he had loved and served, to become its abiding heritage."

We might leave Laurier with that, but as a newspaperman I must offer one more, as O'Leary told it to me:

> When Laurier died (we had been attacking him pretty vigorously over conscription and other things) P.D. Ross came in to me in the morning and said "O'Leary, I want you to write the editorial on Laurier. I can't trust myself to do it right, I got very mad at Laurier and I'm afraid I'd say the wrong things. You do it."
> So I sat down and wrote the editorial. I remember, by God, I remember—how do you start an editorial like that? And I waited and waited. Finally I hit upon a line—and I always liked it myself

—"Today we come in sorrow to speak of Wilfrid Laurier— dead."
Once I had that I was all right, and I wrote about 2,000 words. Well,
P.D. came in that evening to see that editorial; apparently he was a bit
nervous and rightly so. He just came into my room and said: "O'Leary
that's a noble editorial. Do you mind if I just change or add one line?"
All the line was, was a qualification of something I had said: he wrote
that we had hoped that Sir Wilfrid would take the part that the majority
of his country had wished him to take on conscription, that's all.

So it was that at the age of 30 O'Leary wrote the column-and-a-half
editorial of the Conservative *Ottawa Journal* on the great Liberal leader.

Sir Robert Borden

I wonder if O'Leary would have become so ardent a party man had Laurier
been followed by lesser Conservatives than Borden and Meighen, and if
King, the Liberal successor, had been more staunch and stimulating? I think
Laurier's death was to O'Leary the death of honest liberalism. It was to
preserve honest liberalism in its best sense that Grattan became so militant
against not only King, but against old-line, reactionary Tories.

To Carleton University in February of 1967 O'Leary gave what I believe
to be the best address of his career, under the title "Borden, Meighen
—Canadian Nationalists." We'll look first at some of his words on Borden:

Borden took the Canadian Conservative Party from sentimental colonialism to robust Canadian nationalism, did it all but single-handed
and to the consternation of many in his party, some of whom were still
wet with the spray of the deluge. The truth is that with the passing of
Macdonald, the party lapsed into an unashamed colonialism. The old
colonial way and theory did not end with the death of Queen Victoria; it
lasted unchanged until after the First War. The Canadian people, it must
be said, liked it that way. It was the day of Rudyard Kipling, of "Rule
Britannia" and "Soldiers of the Queen"—songs which were on the
covers of our school copy-books. Indeed, so far as our English-
speaking population was concerned, their spiritual home was in London. British Governments were infallible; British Governments could

do no wrong—if it rained in the Strand, the thing to do was to turn up your trouser legs on Sparks Street.

As late as 1918, when Sir Robert Borden held that Canada should have separate representation at the Peace Conference, Mr. W.S. Fielding, for many years Sir Wilfrid Laurier's chief lieutenant, issued a solemn warning against a step which, he said, *"might lead to the danger of making Canada a separate nation."* I was in the Press Gallery when Mr. Fielding made that statement. Not a single Liberal rose to object; not Mr. Ernest Lapointe, not Mr. Charles Gavan Power, not Mr. Rodolphe Lemieux, not a single Liberal on the Union Government side. The one voice that rose to protest and challenge was that of the so-called arch-Imperialist, *Arthur Meighen*. I shall quote his words later on.

Now it must be admitted that, in his early days, Sir Robert Borden belonged to this colonial-minded school. When he made his major speech in defence of his Naval Aid Bill of 1912—an offer of $35,000,000 to the British Admiralty for the building of three dreadnaughts—he ended it with this quotation:

Half-mast our flags?
   Nay, hoist them to the breeze!
We've sown in sacrifice
   And we reap the corn;
See on that African veldt
   An Empire born

(Curiously enough, that quotation was not carried over into the revised Hansard. I have often wondered whether Sir Robert decided that it had too much of corn, or had already begun to repent.)

Certainly there was no question of his repentance later on. In 1917, as a member of the Imperial War Cabinet, he sat down with his friend, South Africa's Jan Christian Smuts, and drafted a momentous resolution to be presented to the British Government.

It demanded for the Dominions the preservation of "all existing powers of self-government . . . complete control of domestic affairs

. . . full recognition of the Dominions as autonomous nations. . . . An adequate voice in foreign policy. . . . continuous consultation in all matters of common Imperial concern. . . . Such necessary concerted action, founded on consultation, as the several governments might determine.''

Borden moved this resolution, Smuts seconded it, and the Lloyd George Government accepted it without a word of objection.

"You and I", said Smuts to Borden—*"You and I have transformed the structure of the British Empire."*

O'Leary recalled that the distinguished Liberal, Senator Charles Gavan Power, had written this of Borden:

Borden in many respects did not receive the full measure of appreciation to which he was entitled as statesman till long after he had retired from public life. . . . It was not understood that in his relations with the United Kingdom authorities he had taken the most advanced stand of any Canadian public man up to that time, and that in matters relating to the employment of Canadian troops. . . . and to Canadian representation at the Peace Conference, he had been almost brutally frank. "We will not always be in the front line and have a back seat at the conference table" was a sentiment that could have brought wild applause if repeated to the most nationalist audience in Quebec. . . . It was only in after years that the Canadian people as a whole learned what manner of man he was.

Summing up, O'Leary said:

Too many Canadians do not realize that it was Borden, standing out from the hierarchy of his own party, and providing true leadership, who laid the foundations for the Statute of Westminster. That it was Borden who first objected to the British Government nominating a Governor General of Canada. That it was Borden who first proposed a Canadian Minister at Washington. That it was Borden who first proposed a

Canadian as Canada's Governor General. That it was Borden who was our first *effective* Canadian nationalist.

I link him with Macdonald and Laurier as one of the three men who were our truly great Prime Ministers.

A Pause for a Laugh

If this book were to proceed in an orderly fashion it would move now to O'Leary's profound admiration, and even awe, of Arthur Meighen. But Grattan would be appalled if people thought of him as a man steeped always in great thoughts on nationhood. He was as lively as a puppydog's tail. Let's look at him as he was about the time he was admiring Borden. I have a frivolous house-edition of *The Journal* printed Dec. 12, 1925, on the paper's 40th anniversary, revealing how ''the wild one'' looked to his colleagues:

Grattan O'Leary breathed his first at a place called Percé, and after an early education in which he learned to extol the merits of everything maritime, he became a Conservative after hearing that Sir John A. spoke better under the influence than over it. . . . Our hero put to sea and learned to list to port and also to sherry. After twenty five years of cruising around Saint John harbor he became a reporter. He was a many-sided reporter and after he had made his mark on many raised cheques he was sentenced to the press gallery. Graduating from the press gallery he became an editorial writer, and to date has freed Ireland from English bondage 650 times by actual count. . . . He was responsible for the rumour that he had contested Gaspé against Speaker Lemieux. With true native grace he refused the demand of his supporters for a recount after it was confirmed. Like all great Celts, he is of medium height, raven hair and raving disposition, slightly knock-kneed and slices badly off the tee. He is a great after-midnight speaker, and will shortly address the Civil Service on important matters such as the ''pork keg.'' His favorite statesman is Arthur Meighen, and it is understood he taught the latter French. That is merely another rumour regarding this many-sided and lopsided man . . . In his youth he was a great boxer and has boxed the compass many a time. His hobbies include the W.C.T.U., which has often discussed him at great length.

Interviewed recently on Mackenzie King, the word "scoundrel" appeared eighteen times and it therefore cannot be used.

Arthur Meighen

And now Meighen. I must try to tell of O'Leary's reverence for the man so it will remain this side of idolatry. That address he gave at Carleton was as much a memorial and creed as it was a speech. Some had called Meighen "a magnificent failure," he said quietly, his hands demurely clasped together before him. Then, banging fist into palm:

> A failure Meighen was if our standard in judging leadership be a man's ability to win votes, to hold on to office. Arthur Meighen believed in political integrity; would not stoop to conquer. I give you one example. When in the election of 1926 his party advisers in Winnipeg told him that if he would come out in favor of the Hudson Bay Railway they could guarantee him six additional seats in Manitoba, his reply to them was: "I do not believe in the Hudson Bay Railway, and I will make no such statement." Surely this is the moral courage, this the mark of true leadership the youth of Canada cry out for today.

Other forms of Meighen's courage sprang from O'Leary's memory. In his first speech in Parliament he assailed tariff protection for manufacturers who made their profits "behind ramparts of gold." He spearheaded the creation of the Canadian National Railways to break down the CPR monopoly. He criticised tired Conservatives, supporting instead Bacon's sayings "It is as well to create good precedents as to honor old ones," and "We must take counsel from both times, from the past what is best, from the present what is fittest." When in 1918 the Liberal W.S. Fielding warned that separate representation for Canada at Versailles might lead to Canada becoming a separate nation, Meighen replied that "as a distinct entity within the British Empire, and as a distinct self-governing entity, we are entitled to a voice in the attitude assumed by Great Britain in the disposal of every question that pertains to the terms of peace."

O'Leary came then in full flight to a point he used often to make, with ever new excitement and pride. At the Imperial Conference of 1921, which O'Leary attended, Meighen opposed renewal of the Anglo-Japanese

Alliance—against Lloyd George, Churchill, Birkenhead, Curzon and Australia's redoubtable William Hughes—and in the end had his way in "a supreme triumph of moral force and power of persuasion." O'Leary summed up: "In that hour it was Arthur Meighen who, almost single-handed, dictated a major foreign policy for the whole British Empire—and without the support of his party's leaders back home."

At the conference, O'Leary recalled, he used to get from Meighen an outline each evening of his position in the discussion. One morning Meighen showed him "with amusement" a cablegram he had received from Sir George Foster, acting Prime Minister, urging him to "keep an eye on O'Leary's despatches, which are misrepresenting your position outra-geously." And later on, a Toronto Conservative newspaper accused Meighen of "treason."

O'Leary gave the Carleton audience Meighen's concept of leadership:

> He did not believe that a Prime Minister or a Party leader should constantly have his ear to the ground, trying to find out what the public wanted, or what it thought it wanted. He held that what is too often mistaken for public opinion is merely propaganda for some special interest. The business of a Prime Minister, or of a Government, or of a party leader, was to get the best advice he could from his expert, from technicians and research specialists, to form a policy upon that advice, and then take it to the people and to fight for it, regardless of the consequences.
>
> The more I see of government—and I have been watching it from a ringside seat for more than 50 years—the more I believe in that.

In support of elitism he drew on his friend Prof. Frank Underhill. "I agree with him that government is the business of the elite; an elite in Parliament and in the higher civil service. In our world today government is too strong a thing to be left to amateurs or to what is called 'public opinion.' " Sir Edward Grey had written in his memoirs that after a quarter of a century in public life he had "come to the conclusion that most of the mistakes made by governments in his time were made because governments thought that public opinion was a great statesman, when the truth was that public opinion was not a great statesman at all." "That is true!" cried out Grattan, "and it is more true today than it was in the time of Sir Edward Grey!"

I dwell on this a moment. O'Leary could often seem to incite or attack with reckless abandon, but the words remained steady, as people who took him on soon found out. In this case, he had not said the public was an ass or not worth listening to. He had said a government must get the best advice it could from experts, form a policy upon that advice, and then take it to the public. He would say it was no part of the duty and responsibility of Parliament to govern by plebiscite, opinion poll or press. He was not cynical about the ability of the public to come to common sense conclusions if it were given the issues in fair perspective.

To return to that Carleton talk: O'Leary summed up his respect for Meighen by saying that "the fortunes of politics were indeed merciless for him, and they robbed us of the full gain of his genius. . . . In the more than half a century that I have known our public life, it has never known a finer intelligence nor a more honest man."

Right up until Meighen's death in 1960 the two remained close friends, as did their families. It was a privilege to see the two chatting together in long reminiscence, not sad, certainly not bitter, but smiling, reflective—and grateful for each other's friendship and the fullness of their lives. I have several Meighen tributes to O'Leary, but this one will do; "Had the ebb and flow of political tides followed each other in periods the reverse of what they did, this man would have become eminent in two spheres of life and would be recognized everywhere as the D'Arcy McGee of this generation."

Defeat at the Polls
One of the tides Meighen had in mind would be that which on October 29, 1925, unceremoniously dumped O'Leary on the shore of the Gaspé Peninsula on the only occasion he ran for Parliament.

Ironically, it was Meighen's doing! He had wanted to get O'Leary into his cabinet and persuaded him to run in Gaspé, his old home constituency. Grattan was off in Australia at an Imperial Press Union Conference when he learned that another candidate had won the Tory nomination. He hustled home, upset the nomination but failed to get the campaign money from the man he replaced. He had vanished. His opponent, too, was tough: the Hon. Rodolphe Lemieux, former Commons Speaker and at that time Liberal House Leader. Lemieux got 7,615 votes, O'Leary 3,528—but Lemieux' previous majority was cut by 3,374 votes. O'Leary laughs now that he hadn't a prayer, but that it was the gayest and worst-handled campaign a would-be MP ever staged. "Lemieux had the friends, he had the money, he knew the tricks—all I could do was make speeches and he could do that better too. But Good God, it was fun!" His old friend Arthur Ford wrote in the London *Free Press* that O'Leary blamed his defeat on the Turks! Meighen had supported Lloyd George's warning that the Turks must leave Macedonia alone, and O'Leary found himself painted in the fishing posts of Gaspé as willing to conscript the sons of Quebec to go off to war against the Terrible Turks. But it was all grist for the mill of the man who was to become an uncrowned Tory money-raiser, high conscience and front-line fighter.

The "Quiet Years"

We now enter in the O'Leary story what appear to be "the quiet years"—from about 1927 until 1939. The period began with Mackenzie King, who bored him, and ended with the onset of World War II, which spurred him to a new surge of advocacy. He did not lose interest in politics, but lacking was the impact he had received from the emotion of Laurier, the quiet courage of Borden, the mind of Meighen. It was a time of consolidation after astonishing ascent.

I did not know him then, really. I was at school until 1929 and after a couple of years as an office boy and cub with *The Journal* I left to join The Canadian Press for eight years, working in many cities in Canada, and New York and London. I didn't see much of him in the early years of the war, either, for I was working with the British Commonwealth Air Training plan. But I have since sensed that, though he was "quiet" in those 14 years, his mind was not fallow but being stored with the riches of literature and friends. I doubt if anyone had ever drawn, or ever will draw, as many books from the Parliamentary Library in any such period as he did then. He was in there so much they rarely logged his borrowings. His returns came in only in cardboard boxes piled in the back seat of a taxi after Martin Burrell or F.A. Hardy, the long-suffering librarians, threatened to send down the Mounties.

They weren't books to him; they were people, the people who wrote them and the people in them. His was a fantastic memory. Some who didn't know him perhaps suspected that his writings and speeches were swotted up "under the lamp." Not so, or very rarely so. Recollections sprang from him as they related to what he was doing or thinking. His banter at cribbage, his mock rage at golf, his writing on the death of a friend, his exasperation in political attack or his musing on a summer verandah—all his talk was warmed and livened not by his own life alone but all who live in books.

How he longed to interest everyone else in books! It was as though he was paying his debt to that Bishop back in the Gaspé. Nevinson, Pope, Willison, Synge, Delane, Chesterton, Montague, Blunt. These and so many more he spurred me to read. If I had written something he might say it was interesting and that I'd enjoy what Mencken had written on the subject, or would find a strong judgment Duff had earlier brought down. I'd discover, of course, that what I had written was but the tip of the iceberg, and when I'd tell him of finding his treasures his happiness was genuine in its shared delight.

In those quiet years he was also able to give more time to friendships. It was a rich experience to hear him talk of friends as he did of books. He'd recall, never boastfully, good times and talk with such as Skelton, Donald Gordon, Brockington, Graham Towers, Angus Macdonald, Stanley McLean, Leo Dolan, Clifford Clark, John McCurdy, Howe; and newspaper friends such as Dafoe, Ferguson, Dexter, Stevenson, Ford, John Bassett Sr., and D.B. McRae, "the best essayist Canadian journalism ever had." His reminiscences were almost invariably on the happy side. There was talk of ill-begotten policies not soon enough forgotten, of official frailties and poor parliaments. But as to individuals, he chose to remember the pleasure of their company. When he did have to be critical it was usually in sorrow: "Ah, the dear man was over his head in that company. . . ." In extremity, "He was an unmitigated disaster and not very honest either, but you know, he did a lot of good things earlier. . . ."

Grattan delighted in paying tribute to his friends. My tape recorder has the sincerity and chuckle of his voice, but here are his *words* on two friends of the quiet years we are looking at:

We have in Ottawa what is known as the Dining Out Club, a small group which meets on the first Tuesday of each month for food and wine and talk. It was started by Sir Lyman Duff some 50 years ago. We prevailed upon Mr. Justice Rand to join us, and I can hardly tell you what a glory it was to have Rand and Duff at the same table, both intellectual giants and two of the best talkers I have ever known. The two men were in many ways different. Duff, I often thought, saw British history in the light of James Anthony Froude, sometimes in traditions that had the color of blood or of numbers left in the field. Only God knows how many expensive linen tablecloths Duff ruined by tracing upon them with a black pencil a map of the Battle of Waterloo—showing us exactly where the Imperial Guard stood at a precise moment, and the very minute of the hour at which Picton attacked. Rand on the other hand, was a social historian; seeing Britain's history through the sufferings, trials and triumphs of the masses, but a loving touch for poetry, music, baseball—and people. Where Duff's heroes of the law were the Currans, the Erskines, the Broughams and the Birkenheads, the legal giants Rand seemed to reverence were North Americans—Brandeis and Holmes and Learned Hand. But I must say that Duff and Rand did have one thing in common—both were tainted with the original sin of Liberalism, and they never quite escaped from it. Duff would recall pridefully how he had stood on the same platform with Edward Blake; and Rand never quite got over an ideological hangover from the days when he stumped for the Liberal party in New Brunswick. I loved them the more for that. Political parties, like my Church and Communism, *do* leave their marks upon people. And hypocrisy has no place in the make-up of judges, anyway.

And Then War

Grattan O'Leary knew the hurt of war—two of his sons went over, Owen not to return; and Brian to be reported missing for a grievous time, but then safe. He rarely spoke of the personal grief, though it added sensitivity to his writing and speaking on the war. His voice was heard not only in his own paper, but across Canada and afar. He was one of a small party of Canadian journalists invited by the British Government to go over early in the war to report on Britain's war effort. He went to Ireland to interview Premier de Valera, he went to London to report the British elections in 1945 which turned out Churchill. During the conflict he was a regular commentator for the CBC, broadcast frequently to Britain for the BBC, and spoke on a wide variety of platforms in Canada and the United States.

What was the beat of the heart of a man who had long deplored war, and who, with Irish forebears, had never been an unquestioning supporter of all things British? At New York in 1941, he addressed the 35th annual convention of the Association of Life Insurance Presidents:

My privilege in being here this morning is increased by the fact that your nation today achieved the heroic distinction of having war declared upon it by Nazi Germany, and achieved the further distinction of having war declared upon you from the vile lips of Benito Mussolini. My privilege in coming here is heightened, too, by the fact that within hours after bombs fell upon Pearl Harbour, my country declared war on the Empire of Japan. We declared war on Japan not merely because the Prime Minister of England had given you a pledge: we declared war as well because we are North Americans, because our destiny, with your destiny, is upon this continent, and because as you had walked with us in our way of life we were resolved to march with you on your path of sacrifice. Upon that path of sacrifice, we shall march with you to the end, bound neither by treaties nor by wish for gain.

You recall the old slurs, the old aspersions, on democracy. You remember how our young intellectuals told us that democracy was decadent; of how it had fumbled and failed: you remember how they said that what we needed was a dictator—a dictator who would hack his way through democratic checks and balances to a greater efficiency.

They are not talking that way now. They are not talking that way now because they have seen that this business of hacking through democratic checks and balances means hacking through human lives and human values—hacking through those things which we of the British tradition have been taught to believe are among the dearest of human possessions.

You, and we, are fighting the Empire of Japan. But you and we are also fighting the Nazi Empire of Adolf Hitler—and in that Empire, across the Atlantic, and not across the Pacific, abides our greatest peril. Unless Adolf Hitler can be destroyed, unless and until the armies of the democracies meet and defeat his legions somewhere in the Old World's soil, victory over Japan must be an empty thing. If we on this continent ignore that truth, if by any faltering of ours we let England down, then we shall invite and deserve the reproach of our children and the indictment of history; invite that saddest of all tragedies in the human story—the epitaph of a vanished liberty.

We of North America, no matter what our problems and our perils here, will not say to her now: *Here are the tools: you go finish the job.*

Reading that now, 33 years later, is one thing. Imagine giving that challenge to a people whose country had just then discovered its soil could be ravaged by enemies from the other side of the world! O'Leary did a number of such tasks for democracy during the war, in Canada, Britain and the United States. After the job had been finished, he addressed the 45th annual meeting of the National Machine Tool Builders Association of the United States, in Quebec City, Oct. 8, 1946. For a few moments he talked of Canada's own war story, and of his hope that this was one of those cases where "a country's past proclaims its future." He continued:

But my friends, wherever you go today you meet people who are bitterly disillusioned about what has come to the world since the end of the war. I am convinced that a great deal of the disillusionment stems from the fact that we gave ourselves certain promises during the war, told ourselves certain things which had birth only in our emotional imaginations. We were fighting for survival; we were fighting for our very lives, but we were not content with that. We told ourselves and we told our soldiers that they were fighting for a brave new world; some new Jerusalem on earth, a sort of paradise in which we would all live gloriously amid magic gadgets. Now, we are discovering something different. Now we are discovering that democracy's victories are never final, that history is perpetual recommencement, that humanity does not take on divinity overnight, and that life at best is a hard campaign with some lost battles.

One wants to let the strength and beauty of that passage stand. But lest a reader find it dispirited, I want to add that the heartbeat of Grattan's life was that he rejoiced that history was always beginning again, and that we had the privilege of striving to make it better, though some battles be lost.

What was he like in the office, this Grattan O'Leary? Now that this narration is up to the late 1940's I have been with him enough to let you glimpse him "as he was."

He used the two-fingered, hunt-and-peck system on a beleaguered old typewriter he wouldn't give up, and he beat the hell out of it at a terrific clip. When in flight his jockey-like body was hunched over the machine, swaying incessantly backward and forward, his face sometimes swooping almost down to the keyboard. Feverishly he'd read the half-sentences as they came out, his lips working at them so his ear would get the music or spacing of the message. If it didn't "read," he'd cross it out with a vicious tattoo on the "x" and "m" keys, and do the sentence again until it did. If he didn't notice you standing in his door during these birthing moments, it would be partly because of the haze rising from the cigarette in his mouth into his eyes; partly for the din of the machine; partly because his thoughts were wholly on the cause he was pleading or damning.

He worked in his vest. The cheap wood typewriter table was black with cigarette burns. Suddenly he'd dart into one of our offices to borrow a cigarette or match, never returning it.

His main desk was a kind of compost heap. A big round pile of stuff, usually 12 or 15 inches high, filled either side of the surface so that in front of him was a valley clear of everything except the clips or notes he was working on for that moment.

The two mounds had no separate purpose. There were personal letters and bleats to the editor; there were household bills and old Racing Forms. There were texts of other men's speeches, sent for praise and receiving the grace of storage treatment prior to oblivion. Sometimes one of us would get an appeal from a high or low source asking couldn't he get an answer to the question he had ages ago written to O'Leary. With optimism born of experience, I'd go in and he'd say: "Oh God, didn't I answer that—here, I know where it is." With that, his hand would not touch either mound but sort of hover over it; and then he would insert thumb and forefinger into the slope and extract it. "You answer it, will you Norman; he's a curious fellow, really, but a dear soul and we should answer him."

Forgetful, yes, but charmingly so. Not infrequently he'd lose his glasses, and call out for an office-boy, give him fifty cents and tell him to go to

Woolworth's "and buy what they call their reading glasses in black frames, they're in a tray on the right hand side."

About twice a year an anxious voice would come on the phone about 12:40 and ask if I knew where O'Leary was. He was due to speak to their club or association. Sometimes he had left two minutes earlier, telling me where he was going. Sometimes he was out in the newsroom yarning with Tom Lowrey, his speech forgotten. Sometimes he had gone, but we knew not where and could only pray. This was amusing to us but rough on audiences, so I worked out a system whereby one of us had always a standby speech on journalism or Canada which we could deliver in a real emergency.

And at the Races

The man who never returned a cigarette was the easiest touch in the office for a loan, to any man in the building. I'm sure he lost on that, but he never pressed anyone. The man who'd forget to go and make his speech almost never had to look up quotations from poets or politicians. He'd just bang it down, and it was almost always right. If someone would write, catching him out, he'd say "Run the letter," and bang his fist against his forehead.

In those days he never had much money but his pocketbook always bulged; for he played cribbage or poker almost daily, and kept his winnings in his pocket lest tomorrow he had to pay 'em out. When they raced horses and not buggies at Connaught Park he had still further need for folding cash. He had lost money on most every nag on the continent, but being there with him was a picnic. His back was hunched with hunches: if a jockey's colour was yellow and Grattan had on a yellow tie—that was enough. One day a lady in our group asked him to put five dollars for her on a cripple's nose. Knowing it couldn't run for its life, Grattan didn't place her bet, and of course was going to return her five dollars. It won. He gave her $40 after pretending to cash the ticket. As I had not seen him at the wicket I questioned him, aside. He said, "Now don't you say a word, Norman, I'll win it back next race anyway."

Of His Craft

He was better on a typewriter. In 44 years in many newspaper offices I've never seen such consistently clean copy as came from O'Leary. He would chisel and shape with the caring of a craftsman, and once it seemed right he would laboriously retype the many parts that had been hacked up with editing marks. Absurd to him would be the current idea that a writer should just sit down and let his subconscious roll out to help the great tide of human thought.

I was not in the least responsible for his art and skill, but for years it was part of my job to see all the copy of our team, to edit or question its content. That is not always a pleasant task, for we writers tend to fancy our writing. But taking a suggestion to Grattan was easy. It seemed to delight him to see that we cared! He made writing and editing a game, as others might argue over which fly to use on a dark day, or whether a pitching wedge is more useful than a nine-iron. "Glad you spotted that," he said to me one time, "it's a funny thing about writing—you forget the reader can't know what you have in mind unless you say it."

I've seen him come in in the morning and wave from the door, "I've got the word we were looking for. . . ." He'd tell me with a chuckle how he had got thinking about it the night before; and with luck, his talk would go on to personal recollections of the right word used by a great poet or author in a certain instance and how he had never forgotten it. Out would come the quotations, recited there in full heart, from poetry or R.B. Bennett or a yarn on golf by Bernard Darwin. He loved words, loved to weigh them for sound as well as for sense, loved seeking the right one instead of one that would do.

He was also a bear for work, though that is not the way to say it. His work was his life, his life was his work. He believed a newspaper should concern itself with every phase of life, and he used weekends to broaden his vigil. Monday morning he'd place a book on my desk, exclaiming "I read this over the weekend and have written a piece about it—I think you'll enjoy the book specially the letters." On saying which, he'd move quickly to his office and in no time you'd hear the typewriter going on something else he would have been thinking about over the weekend: arguing with something in the New York *Sunday Times* (which he always read), commenting on a Belloc quote in the *New Statesman* and *Nation*, or venting a printable curse at the travesty that was Friday's prizefight, recalling the great days of fights as though he had spent his life in arenas and poolrooms. There was only one challenge in journalism he knew nothing about—the problem of finding something to write about each day.

I want to say something, too, of the "attitude to work" he showed to us all by example, without his being aware of it. When the New York *Herald Tribune* folded he wrote an article recalling its flair and character, but then discovered we had already used a two column piece from the AP. "Throw mine out, the AP's got all my facts and did a better job on the old-timers who wrote for the paper." I demurred, but he insisted. When Frank Underhill died in 1971 I phoned Grattan to see if he would do a personal recollection. He sent it over with a note saying "My pen is rusty" and asking me to chuck it away if it wasn't right. One day I put on his desk a political editorial which I had written; it was full of invective, and I attached a note: "Okay, so I'm mad; if too mad and too long I'll cut it." He read it and banged back a memo: "So you're mad! Pulitzer said any editorial writer who didn't see something in the paper that made him damned mad wasn't worth a damn. I go for every word of this." One night about midnight when I was leaving, after writing a signed column on a Commons blow-up, Grattan was coming in to do an editorial.

"Did you get your piece done, Norman?"

"Yes, but I'm kind of worried about it."

"Good; if you weren't worried about it, I would be."

And, oh God yes, after I was "grown up" he handed back an editorial I had submitted, saying sternly but quietly: "Norman, this is too long and too confused, and it mixes frivolity and seriousness in a way that won't do. But what really worries me about it is that you know it has these faults but didn't work them out of it. That's all I'm going to say." And he walked out.

The man made a kind of career encouraging all of us—and I was the luckiest. He would urge the paper to send me to cover a U.S. election, to cover a conference in Geneva or Quebec City, to do a feature piece on the Louis-Schmeling fight, and so on. He'd ask me to go to a local meeting of some kind because "I'd like you to get to know that crowd." And though our habit was never to say who wrote editorials, for they were unsigned, I sometimes heard he had told people I had written one. "Hell, they were congratulating *me* on it!"

Yes, working with and for Grattan O'Leary was an experience all of us cherished. He'd reach out—whether we were at home or away on assignment—to tell us we had done a good job. And when we didn't there was no beating about the bush: "What on earth ever made you think that?" This was the O'Leary we loved. Then there was the O'Leary we respected—the man who stood for the best in newspaper ethics and principles.

His Newspaper Principles

Though the best-known of the three, Grattan O'Leary always said, generously but I think genuinely, that most of his principles in journalism he had acquired from P.D. Ross and my father. Long after their deaths he would often guide or end a discussion of some problem with the comment: "Well, I always remember old P.D. saying . . ." or, "You know, Mr. Smith used to draw a hard line against this sort of thing. I remember once. . . ." As we have examined both the Ross and Smith creeds of journalism, we need not portray them again. But Grattan more than either of them set down in moving, urgent language what should be the role of a newspaper for people, parliament and nationhood. I want to preserve what the man said on these matters.

Freedom of the Press

Freedom of the press was, of course, at the root of most of the utterances. When on June 28, 1965, the Senate was discussing the Government's proposed favorable treatment to the American magazines *Time* and *Reader's Digest*, O'Leary made a memorable analysis of what Freedom of the Press is—and what it isn't:

> All that press freedom means is that the right of free speech has been extended to the printing press, nothing less and nothing more. And that right of the printing press is enjoyed by some little printer in a garret, just as surely as it is enjoyed by the powerful publisher of the greatest newspaper. It is the printing press alone, not some newspaper, which has been granted freedom in these matters. I never thought you could give some reporter a writing pad and pencil, and send him down the street and invest him with some special significance. This is nonsense. I have been attending newspaper meetings in Canada for years, and have heard newspapermen rise and quote that poetic declamation of Milton:

Give me the liberty to know, to utter and to argue according to my conscience, above all other liberties.

That, as I said, was a splendid poetic declamation, but if you look at it carefully you will find that no more unintelligent and no looser statement has ever been written in the English language. Give me the right, according to my conscience, to utter treason! Give me the right, according to my conscience, to utter language endangering the security of the state, to incite to riot! Give me the right, as Mr. Justice Holmes put it, to rise in a crowded theatre and shout "Fire!"

Then you hear newspapermen speaking about the terrible danger of taxing advertising. Advertising has been taxed in this country for years on end. Newspapers are not immune from the laws of Government or municipalities: they never have been, and they never can be. Practically everything that goes into the production of a newspaper is taxed, but what in the name of common sense has this to do with freedom of the press? The doctrine of the freedom of the press never guaranteed the profits of a newspaper, and it never intended that the publisher should have some special dispensation from the ordinary laws of the nation.

Hate Literature

A commodity that O'Leary would instinctively find revolting and sick is Hate Literature. But see how he developed the spacious theme that to ban even hate literature is a doubtful and even dangerous step! On May 5, 1970, the Senate was debating an amendment to the Criminal Code to curb the stuff. O'Leary said, in part: "I know all about hate literature. . . .

We all get these papers. But after all, what has been the consequence? The consequence over a number of years has been the ecumenical movement. The consequences over the years has been greater understanding between Christians and Jews. Intelligent, educated Christians have not believed, and do not believe, in the Protocols of Zion. I do not think that intelligent non-Catholics believe in the alleged Knights of Columbus Oath.

Honourable Senators, the only sure cure for this kind of thing is the better education of our people. When people are educated and when they become civilized, they become immune to this sort of thing, and I honestly believe that our Canadian people have become immune to it. . . . You cannot by law stop people lying; you cannot by law stop people being bigots; you cannot by law, I am sure, stop people from circulating hate literature; but you can stop it by a higher degree of education among our people. . . . This Senate . . . is supposed not only to help put good laws on the statute books, but . . . to prevent bad laws going on the statute books.

Bordering on Censorship

About the War Measures Act, and in a sense about censorship, O'Leary addressed the Senate on Oct. 27, 1970—at the time of the disorders in Quebec:

Let me say at the beginning, without reservation and without equivocation, that I support absolutely and wholeheartedly the resort to the War Measures Act in the circumstances that existed. . . . We cannot condone murder. Any society that condones the hideous sort of crime that was committed in the Province of Quebec ten or fifteen days ago is erecting its own gallows. The Government had no other resort, (but) in saying that I do hope that the Prime Minister will, in administering the act, have regard to what he wrote only three years ago in his introduction to *Federalism and the French Canadians*: "The oldest problem of political philosophy . . . is to justify authority without destroying the independence of human beings in the process. . . . Too much authority, or too little, and that is the end of freedom."

Honorable Senators, there is a dark and misty area in the situation over the past three weeks that needs answers by the Government, with clarity and candour. Last week he (the Prime Minister) repudiated Mr. Marchand, and yesterday in the other place he repudiated Mr. Turner. Mr. Trudeau said: "No; you have all the facts. There are no other facts to disclose. I will disclose no further facts." He adds to this by saying that in that position the Government will stand or fall. . . . Of course the Government stands or falls, but it stands or falls only after the people in possession of all the facts are in a position to decide whether it should stand or fall. That is our system. Mr. Trudeau can say, "Oh well, you can turn me out later." But that is not our system. He is not sitting in the Kremlin; he is sitting in the Parliament of Canada and he is accountable. If you can invoke an act such as the War Measures Act, one of the most extraordinary acts taken in the history of this country outside of wartime, then surely the duty devolves upon you to tell the people why you had to do it.

The Magazine Business

On Sept. 16, 1960, the Royal Commission on Publications was directed, by John Diefenbaker's government, "to make recommendations to the Government as to possible measures which, while consistent with the maintenance of the freedom of the press, would contribute to the further development of a Canadian identity through a genuinely Canadian periodical press." O'Leary was appointed Chairman, and made commission history by reporting on May 25, 1961. He enjoyed every exciting and boring moment of the hearing of evidence—but the result was disappointing.

In the Senate on June 28, 1965, he had occasion to look back at the hearings, this way:

> Our sole aim was to try to secure a climate of competition in which Canadian publications, serving Canada worthily in a vital area, should have a chance to survive . . . We found, in brief, that Canadian periodicals were in fact subject to competition, unfair, unjust and crippling. I am not going to weary you tonight with statistics of what are known as "split runs" or "regional editions" or even "overflow circulation," but I do want to deal briefly with what are known as Canadian editions represented by *Time* magazine and *Reader's Digest*. A Canadian edition, so-called, is a periodical whose editorial content is lifted in whole or in large part, from a parent edition outside Canada, and then used in Canada to attract Canadian advertising. In other words, outside or foreign editorial matter is dumped into Canada. The truth is that the printing of "Canadian editions" is not a publishing endeavor at all; it is an importing business.
>
> We therefore defined a Canadian periodical as one published in Canada, owned either by Canadian citizens or, if a corporation, by a

company incorporated under the laws of Canada or one of its provinces, and which is controlled and directed by Canadian citizens and is not a licensee of or otherwise substantially the same periodical owned or controlled outside Canada.

And our main recommendation on that basis was that the deduction from income by a taxpayer of expenditures incurred for advertising directed at the Canadian market in a foreign periodical wherever printed be disallowed.

I ask you to note that the only interest affected by this recommendation was the businessman who dumps cheaply obtained editorial matter on the domestic market, thus diverting by cut-rate prices Canadian domestic advertising from Canadian media. But the right to own a press, and to print and distribute from it whatever is permissible under the law, was in no way trespassed. The commission's recommendations involved no regulation of the preparation, content or free-flow of the editorial material of foreign periodicals; the reader was in no way denied the periodical of his choice.

Honourable senators, I ask you to note clearly what has happened. What has happened is that the Government, by this legislation that is proposed here tonight, and approved by the Commons, has accepted the principle of our commission's recommendations, and then proceeded to make a mockery of the principle—to strangle the principle in its cradle.

They say that deduction from income by a taxpayer of expenditures for advertising in a foreign periodical shall be disallowed; but then, almost in the next breath, they go on to exempt *Time* and *Reader's Digest*, the two principal perils to Canadian periodicals, despite all that the distinguished senator said, and, in effect, to confer Canadian citizenship, for the practical purposes of this law, upon Mr. Henry Luce of New York City, and upon Mr. Dewit Wallace of Pleasantville, New York. These two gentlemen, owners of the so-called Canadian editions I have been describing, are in effect issued Canadian passports—given a green light to go ahead with their destruction of our Canadian periodicals. . . .

Mr. Henry Luce says, "I do not consider *Time* a Canadian magazine.'' This legislation says it is a Canadian magazine, and grants it all the benefits accordingly. More than that, not only are these two magazines exempt from this law, they are entrenched in their present position.

As someone remarked in the other place last week, they have locked the hen-coop door, but they have left two of the biggest foxes inside.

In the Senate Committee on Mass Media hearing of Feb. 17, 1970, the Chairman, Hon. Keith Davey, volunteered that the O'Leary Commission's forecasts of 1961 about the growth of *Time*, for example, ''have been confirmed in the extreme.'' *Time*'s circulation in Canada, said Davey, ''has doubled since 1959 and its advertising has more than doubled.'' O'Leary refused to gloat, but, rather, remarked wryly that *Time* had perhaps become ''the best Canadian magazine we have today.'' As to our truly Canadian publications, ''I must say I have no praise for existing Canadian magazines;'' though he thought *Maclean's* under Peter Newman was getting better. This was perhaps the first indication that O'Leary was becoming weary of the whole magazine affair. With sadness and anger, he said: ''What I am complaining about I blame on the failure not only of one party but of both, because the Conservative Government was not going to accept my report either . . . Somebody once said that if Moses had been a Royal Commission, the Israelites would still be in Egypt.'' On the essence of his report he made one last cry: ''We didn't interfere with press freedom as they call it. We didn't stop American magazines from coming in here. We only said: If they come in here as they are published at home, very well. But if they change them, change their character and merely make them carriers of packaged advertising for the Canadian consumer, we would not let them in, and we advocated a change in the tariffs for that reason.''

To Davey et al

To the Senate Committee on Mass Media, Feb. 19, 1970, his 82nd birthday, came a tousled-haired, textless Senator who made no formal opening remarks except to say, ''Fire away.'' We have already touched on many of the main points O'Leary made in reply to questions, but two things remain. He recognized the press had faults, but it was radio and television coverage of what was going on right there in the Parliament buildings that bugged him most at that moment:

There is an Alice-in-Wonderland quality in communications that we hear night after night. I have convinced myself that today through television we are getting superficiality, we are getting false dimensions of reality, and we are getting matters which confuse and mislead the public. I must say that it disturbs me and frightens me to see reporters—they call themselves newsmen now—reporters out in the hallways of Parliament sticking microphones into the faces of politicians and getting them to say things off the cuff and off the top of their heads. This goes on day after day, and you are coming now to the point where television seems to be more important than Parliament—not what they are communicating but how they are doing it. People don't sit down before the television—not all of them—to listen. They sit down to look and what they hear, or think they hear, is gone with the wind. This is the difference between television and print. You can check print but you can't check television . . . I listen to *Viewpoint*, for example. If you want to be frightened, really, not so much by misrepresentation but by superficiality and sheer ignorance, then listen to . . . some underpaid university professors going on TV and telling you in eight minutes what is wrong with the whole universe and what we should do to correct its behavior.

He was no less tough on newspapers, specially, and I think rightly, on the claim by some reporters that they have a right to protect (conceal) their sources of information if they are brought to court for defamation or inquiry:

This is dangerous nonsense. He says "I have the same rights as the priest in the confessional or I have the same rights as a doctor with his patients." The priest doesn't walk out of the confessional and indict the man who confessed to him, and the doctor doesn't go out and tell the public how one of his patients contracted syphilis. When you put power like that into the hands of an individual—the power to ruin a man's character, his reputation, his place in the community—you are putting dangerous power in the hands of those men. What if he has no sources?

Some marginal notes by the author
Before leaving the hearings of what became known as the Davey Committee I might summarize in two pages my own answers to some of its questions when I was asked to come before them Jan. 22, 1970.

"Would newspaper groups grow?" they asked. "With regret, I expect so, but if a reasonable and democratic way of checking their growth can be devised, I suspect Parliament and people would like to consider it."

"Are groups socially desirable?" they asked: "We all live every day amid things we wish were different. Ideally the country should have a hundred good newspapers under a hundred different publishers and editors, all of these able, without subsidy, to serve their community and country. But in today's conditions could anything short of government subsidy, which too is socially undesirable, enable them all to survive? I don't think so."

I said I did not believe it was in the public interest that one owner or one company should blanket the field of communications in one area through control of all or a dominant portion of its press, radio and television.

I said I believed freedom of the press was no more than the public right of every person to have access to the facts that concern him, and to state his opinion and hear the opinions of others. But the press should be responsible and in effect earn and re-earn its freedom every day—from the public. Freedom of the press was a public freedom, not just a press freedom, and the public should zealously guard it.

I disagreed with some contentions that the committee's study was an invasion of the freedom of the press. We dish it out, we should be able to take it. The press should be under continual public scrutiny.

I thought it essential that Canadian newspapers be Canadian-owned. If the power of the press is termed the Fourth Estate after Sovereign, Parliament and People, then surely this implied Canadian citizenship.

I did not *oppose* the establishment of press councils and did not feel they would necessarily be an infringement on freedom of the press. But I doubted they would do much good, and said they might even provide an umbrella of respectability on newspapers which should on their own want to put out even better papers than any Council could have the power to demand or request. "But all who would 'improve' the press, including this committee, should be wary lest with the best intentions they insert the wedge of government influence that could become control. Aroused public concern and criticism would best improve us."

In conclusion: "If some of us are making more money than is good for us, tax us. If we gang up or monopolize against the public interest, crack down. If we are seditious or libelous or otherwise unlawful, hale us into court. But as to what we put in our papers—good, bad, indecent or incomplete—let the public be the judge. Men of politics should not shape the press. Not if it is to be free."

In the reflective mood of retirement my concern with the media is not in its ability or its principles or its dedication, but that it is flooding the ordinary citizen with more than he can bear, let alone digest. Too much news and too quickly. As to speed, I like the whimsical comment of a man at a ceremony in London a few years ago at the opening of a new communications channel between India and England. He wondered whether India and England and had all that much to say to each other in that much of a hurry! As to quantity, not just in fun I told the Senate Committee the trouble with our press is that Canada has too many trees! If newsprint were more scarce, we'd use words more sparingly, write better, use only good pictures, take more care with make-up, leave less ink on the bedspread and delight the hearts of all newsboys and garbagemen. The best edited and most thoroughly read newspaper in my time, day for day, was the *Times* of London during the severe newsprint rationing in World War Two.

His Political Principles

Grattan O'Leary's "political principles" related to every phase of the phrase: to the science and art of government, to political affairs, to political life and, yes, to a rowdy arena. Raids into the hustings were to him the sweat and energy essential to make idealism work. We have sensed his feelings through his writings on Laurier, Meighen and Borden. Let's now examine his own creed, for which, as someone has said, he was now a crusader, now as an enraged bull and now with a holy fire.

On Oct. 17, 1962, the editor who had "lived" politics all his life made his maiden speech in the Senate. I was there and will not forget it. He had had a cold, and he was nervous. It was one thing to speak to small groups or mass gatherings, but another to speak to Parliament. He began slowly. His notes were only a few scribbled headings. As he picked up confidence, the excitement and the cold fogged his glasses so they became a kind of baton, now on, now off, now a weapon to strike with, now folded quietly and extended as a peace offering. This was the Grattan I knew, and I relaxed. He was not, from then on, a stranger new to the house, but a man who had come home. The senior member of the Senate at that time had been appointed in 1926, but O'Leary began reporting and watching that House in 1912. "I remember the days" he said, "when Sir Richard Cartwright was Government leader and I have a very vivid recollection of Sir George Ross being brought into this chamber in a wheelchair, and speaking powerfully and dramatically from that wheelchair against Sir Robert Borden's naval aid bill of 1912—a speech which in fact resulted in the bill's rejection."

Within two minutes he warned them he did not plan to fit easily into "an atmosphere of relaxed and civilized sophistication," free of the "strident partisanship" of the other house or the newspaper world. Quite the opposite:

> I am a party man, I am a partisan, I am a Conservative without prefix or qualifications. I believe in the two-party system. More than that, I believe that much of the political uncertainty and instability in this country at the present time stems from the fact that too many Canadians have forgotten what the party system is about, and too many Canadians have gone about year after year scoffing at it and deriding it. I have not come into this chamber to turn myself into a political eunuch, and I have no intention of running about with those people with open minds, some of their minds so open that their brains fall out. The principle of democracy is the right of choice, but also, and more important, it is the burden of choice, the responsibility of standing up and being counted.

The House was attentive, and, for the Senate, the galleries had a fair gathering of people who had heard he was going to speak. It happened to be the debate on the Throne Speech, read by the Governor General for Mr.

Diefenbaker. In subsequent years O'Leary described Liberal Throne Speeches variously as a mishmash of platitudes, thin, intangible, unsubstantial vapour, not a program but a yawn. But in his maiden speech and under a Conservative Government, he bore a different toga. "I wonder what people want in a Speech from the Throne. Do they honestly believe any government, Liberal or Conservative or of any other stripe, can at this time in the context of our world come forth with a program guaranteed to cure quickly all the ills that afflict us? This is an evil superstition of our time. . . ." With relish, his cold forgotten, he went on to lash at the Common Market, defend Tory economic policies, and, with obvious delight, declare his colors, vivid and fade-proof. No one slept in the Senate that half hour.

It was not that he was putting on this ardency in politics just because he had been named a Senator. Go back six years, and hear him lecture a crowd of high business people at the annual meeting of the Dominion Mortgage and Investments Associations, in Toronto May 3, 1956. He told them they must think of their responsibilities not to the dollar but to society, and they must not say they are not interested in politics.

> Politics, that is our way of life. That is its foundation, its base. That is the thing which makes democracy today the system which you talk about. That is the shield, the safeguard, the lifeblood of the system which we say we believe in, that we want to defend. But we are not interested in politics!
>
> My friends, that is a terrifying fact in this country. There are some people who think they are too good or too rich or have too exclusive a social family background to soil their patrician hands in the ordinary chores of democracy, men who wouldn't be found dead at a meeting nominating a candidate for parliament or for one of our legislatures, men who never appear at political meetings, and some of whom—and I know some of them in Ottawa as my fellow club members—who would never dare to go out with the mob and just vote. A very famous English poet, Henry Nevinson, a man who spent his life fighting for freedom and democracy, summed up that sort of person in these bitter but true words: "freedom's hypocrites, whose zeal is spent in praising distant freedom; cultured minds of careful ease, that pass and wag the head."
>
> Gentlemen, you can't solve the problems of democracy by merely

muttering slogans or wearing on your buttonhole the latest pin of the newest league; and you certainly can't solve its problems as some of our churches and our service clubs and our newspapers try to solve them, by every five years exhorting people to get out and vote. You just can't make an effective citizen by sending a boy scout after him to vote. Our job is to get people to work at democracy, to try to understand government and its problems every day of every year.

The Senator was an instant partisan in that maiden speech, but he bided his time before telling it what it should do. His first substantial specific challenge was on Sept. 1, 1968. O'Leary recalled that years earlier the Hon. Clifford Sifton had declared the real function of the Senate should be to protect the public from the growing power of the bureaucracy. But now in 1968 the problem was much worse. "The Prime Minister of Canada today wields as much, if not more power than the President of the United States. . . . The real Government of Canada today is carried on from the office of the Prime Minister and the office of the Privy Council. I could name ten bureaucrats having more power than any member of this Chamber or any member of the other place, and far more power in the Government of Canada than any member of the cabinet. The question is, how do we check that growing power? How does the cabinet know it is getting the right advice?"

The Senator was not out on a witch hunt. In countless events he had written and spoken in the highest terms of the civil service and was the first to honor the fact that when governments changed in Canada the great strength and wisdom of the civil service enabled things to go on smoothly as the new team played itself in. What the cabinet needed was some kind of a devil's advocate to check the advice it got from the civil servants:

> I am not saying these men are dishonest, I am not saying they are incompetent, I am not saying they are not good Canadians; but these men are human, they are not infallible. So, there should exist in the cabinet or near the cabinet or in the office of the Prime Minister, some countervailing check on the pretensions and the power of the bureaucracy. Unless this be so, unless this comes, not only the power of the executive, not only the power of the cabinet but the power of Parliament itself will steadily diminish.

O'Leary suggested a role for the Senate in all this:

> Honourable senators, I believe the Senate could play a much more
> effective role than it is playing today. After all, how is the Government
> of this country carried on? I venture to say that 75% of all the ad-
> ministrative acts taken by the Government are taken by order in coun-
> cil. How many of those orders in council are examined by this Senate?
> Do we take a second look at them? How much examination do we give
> to delegated authority, to the acts of bureaux and commissions and so
> on, to the acts of people who are dealing directly with civil liberties,
> dealing with individuals, who can curtail and abuse their power, who
> can abuse the rights of the citizen? This house is supposed to protect
> minorities—and in this case the public is a minority, it is a minority in
> the case of government, in the case of bureaucrats, in the case of
> boards, bureaux and commissions. This house should and could per-
> form a meaningful service, by taking a look at the orders and the
> records of those boards. I submit to you that in no other way will we get
> meaningful parliamentary and democratic government in this land.

He returned to the charge on Dec. 11 of that year, scolding that parliament
and people seemed to be all for speed and no control. "I would never
consent," he said, to the suggestion the Government should introduce bills
in the Senate prior to their going to the Commons. See his words:

> I am disturbed about this theme which runs through this House, through
> the other place and in the press, about speeding up the work of
> Parliament. Parliament is not a legislative mill; Parliament is not a
> production line turning out statutes as General Motors turns out motor
> cars. Parliament, basically, is a place of accountability, a place to
> check the Queen's estimates and to hold the executive to account as to
> how it is carrying on the business of the country . . . If you are going to
> have the Government introduce legislation in this chamber, then this
> chamber will lose entirely its historic character of being a place of
> second thought, a place to review government legislation. I am not
> afraid of the slowness of Parliament. I am afraid that all we are getting

is too many laws on our statute books. The job of this house is not to compete with the House of Commons in putting more laws on our statute books; its job is to see that bad laws do not get on the statute books.

About French Canadians

I think it fair to say that Grattan O'Leary was anxious about the future of French-English relations in this country. He is not one of those aged philosophers who assure us that if we do nothing about it, the problem will go away. I don't think he has ever said so in public, but I suspect he fears and perhaps believes that the worst is still ahead. For that he blames both sides. Conservatives as a party have not done very well by French Canadians and the French Canadians have returned the compliment at the polls. But O'Leary is a man of wide horizons. In the Senate, Nov. 24, 1970, he was criticising the French leaders rather than the people themselves.

He said of English extremists, "Good God, they are betraying their ignorance." And of French Canadians he said there was too much tendency among themselves and their media to blame the Anglo-Saxons and Americans:

I remember the governments of Marchand, of Parent, of Taschereau, of Godbout and Duplessis. These men were all French Canadians, all elected overwhelmingly by French Canadians. They had complete power to deal with wages and hours of labour in the province. Yet when I was a young boy, in the little hamlet of Percé, a bell summoned the workers at dawn to go out on the fishing flakes, to trawl out fish to be dried on the flakes. They were given an hour for lunch and they worked on until dark, and often were summoned out again to work until midnight. These people received, as I remember it, about 75 cents a day.

Why on earth was there no intervention by the government of Mr. Marchand, the government of Mr. Parent, or Mr. Godbout or Mr. Taschereau or Mr. Duplessis? Were they completely unconcerned with the lives of their own people? This went on year after year.

But, honourable senators, there was more than that. There was

Mother Church—and when I speak of Mother Church I speak of my own Catholic church. Mother Church did nothing whatsoever to relieve the problems of these people, to ease their poverty, to ease deprivation of the ordinary things of life, yes, or even to ease degradation and help to heighten the dignity and worth of the individual.

I am not attacking the clergy of Quebec. Most of them were good people—I am sure many of them were holy people; but so concerned were they with life in the next world they failed to concern themselves in the least degree with life in this world. Yes, from Quebec City to Gaspé they dotted the landscape of Quebec with church spires, but you would search in vain from Quebec City to Gaspé to find a public library. This was not a question of Liberals or Conservatives. It happened under Mr. Duplessis, too. It is true that he encouraged and brought in Anglo-Americans with their investments in Quebec. He did a great deal, but he failed to try to prepare his people for change, to make them aware what was happening in the changing world and to prepare them for the new life that was coming to Quebec.

I am certain this has brought about the condition in Quebec today where you have this spirit of lawlessness and young people blaming their adversities upon Anglo-Saxons. Yet I do not despair of Quebec. I do not accept in the least degree that the majority of the people of Quebec are in favor of separatism. No English Canadian should think of separatism. Yet I hear English Canadians say, "Let them go." Good God, they are betraying their ignorance of the history of Canada. This country cannot afford to lose Quebec. It would be an apostasy to our history; it would be a retreat from greatness and a betrayal of our future if we ever lost Quebec.

We observed his words in the Senate asserting that in the crisis of 1970 the Government was right to invoke the War Measures Act, but wrong to withhold so much information. See what he said then about the French in our country:

There are people who go about saying this sort of thing could only happen in the Province of Quebec. I read one of our pundits this week who wrote that the flower of democracy always was a fragile growth in Quebec. Did democracy have a fragile growth when George Etienne Cartier stood side by side with John A. Macdonald at the very cradle of Confederation? Was it a fragile flower that gave us Wilfrid Laurier, who was and remains one of the glories of our nation? Did it have a fragile growth with Ernest Lapointe? Did it have a fragile growth with Georges Vanier?

French in the Public Service

On the vexed question of French in the Public Service—an extremely sensitive matter in Ottawa—O'Leary was caught between his two rooted desires: to maintain the calibre of the Service and to give equal opportunity to all. He faced it squarely. So squarely that the partisans on either side felt he just sat on the fence. I think not, but let's look at the Hansard of June 21, 1972. Under discussion was the intention of Mr. John Carson, Public Service Commissioner, to make the Service more representative of the two founding races. O'Leary says:

> I think Mr. Carson's position is absurd. Of course, we all want our civil service to be representative of all the races in this country, but how do you achieve that? When he says "We will make it representative," does not that involve a quota system? How do you make a distinction between a representative system and a quota system? The merit system is based and must be based on the simple proposition that you hire the man best capable of doing the job, and, honorable senators, you simply cannot do that under a quota system. . . .
>
> I glory in the French fact in Canada. I hope it will continue; I pray it will continue. I am saying that I want French Canadians and Canadians of any other race to have full access to civil service jobs in Canada. However, giving them full access is not to say that we should move to an equal quota system. Of course, they should have access. But if they lack training, if they lack the capacity to do the job in this age of technology where a lot of skill is required then, no matter what their racial origin is, they should not be given the job. This applies to English-speaking Canadians as well as French-speaking Canadians.

The merit system is the merit system, and if we start tampering with it and frittering it away we will lose it. I say God help the Civil Service of Canada if we lose the merit system.

On Youth—and Education

Grattan O'Leary cared a great deal about the young. He seemed to understand them—and they him; in mind he remained one of them. The faults in our approach to education, and his distress at the cynicism of youth were major parts of four addresses between 1946 and 1973. The first of these was to that American Convention of National Machine Tool people. He went right at them by saying that the real danger in education in the United States and Canada was the belief that technical instruction was in some way connected with education. Germany knew all about technical instructions, he said, and we know that Germany wasn't educated. He went on:

> True education, is something of the spirit, something of the inner man, something that brings in a nation of reverence for learning, the thing that made Scotland the great missionary of scholarship. Education is contact with all the great minds of the past. Education is sympathy with your fellow man. Education is love of beauty, love of truth for its own sake. Education is understanding of life, and of life everlasting. Education is sportsmanship. Your great philosopher, Henry James, said that without sportsmanship there could be no democracy. It is sportsmanship, it is mercy, it is love, it is compassion, it is pity. Without that kind of education a nation's future is blurred indeed.

That was the ideal, but it didn't work out. By 1969 a sadness crept into his concern about the young. The Senate on Dec. 19 was discussing the Company of Young Canadians as it was set up by the Federal Government. "For Heaven's sake," he cried; "this is a parliamentary country. If these young people really wanted to make a contribution in Canada, their task, their job, was to join one of our political parties and make a contribution in that way. It is not enough to say that you are an idealist if you are preaching nonsense. These young men should have been told by our leaders and by our schools and by our clergymen what democracy is about. It means getting down to the hard tasks of government in the hard and stony places of the human spirit. When our educational authorities realize that we will avoid in future, I hope, the nonsense of a Company of Young Canadians being given money and free rein to do what they thought was right."

But he didn't concentrate his fire on "the authorities," he let young people and the Young Canadians have it, too:

The mistake young people are making is in their belief that if you come later you must be wiser, (and in) their disrespect and disregard for the past. I hear young men going around sneering at what they call "professional politicians." Not long ago, when speaking at a university, a young man from the audience said to me, "We have respect for public men. What we disrespect are professional politicians." I replied to him this way. "Young man, do you know who the professional politicians were? Burke, who is always on your lips, was a professional politician. He gave up to party what was meant for mankind. Canning, Pitt, Fox, Gladstone, Disraeli and the immortal Churchill, all were professional politicians. We come to the United States, and who is there but Abraham Lincoln, the glory of freedom and democracy. He was a professional politician. So also was Daniel Webster, Henry Clay and Calhoun.

"Then come to your own country. Who were the people who made this Confederation? They were professional politicians. If Confederation had been left to the young people in Canada, regardless of their ideals, or had been left to lawyers, doctors, businessmen and such people, Confederation would never have taken place. It was left to John A. Macdonald, a pro to his very core, and to George Etienne Cartier, a pro to his very core. It was left to Thomas D'Arcy McGee and the others. These were the men who built Confederation, just as professional politicians in England were the men to build up the Empire, which is now the Commonwealth. For heaven's sake, let us not tolerate this continuous smearing of public men and politicians."

A year later he took his message to youth itself, out campaigning, you might say. At that ceremony in which they changed the name of Waterloo University to Wilfrid Laurier University, Nov. 1, 1973, he asked the Chancellor if he might address his closing words to the young people who were present. In the excitement of a political speech O'Leary would wave his arm and slam his fist into his hand, roaring defiance. But when he was talking from some inner creed, he would talk so quietly you scarce could hear him. I wasn't there, but I'm certain this message to the young people before him came in that manner:

We live in a day when old moorings are drifting, when old fighting faiths are being challenged, when cynicism is abroad in the land; the "strong, silent men" extolled, and Parliament dismissed as the "talking shop on the hill."
Let us not despise words:

Words whose transcendent meanings have called
    up the best passions of bygone times,
Steeped through with tears of triumph or remorse,
Sweet with all sainthood,
Cleansed by martyr fires.

Yes, words which, from Pericles to Lincoln, and from Lincoln to Churchill, have been the mightiest of all things in preserving human liberty.

And try to avoid joining in those superficial, senseless and often cruel attacks upon politics and public men. We have good men in Ottawa, and bad, and while some of the pages of history they have made for us we would gladly wipe out, it still remains true, and the most cynical interpretation of history cannot deny, that most of them cared for the common good.

Those who hold differently betray illiteracy, and I think they invite peril. They beckon the evil that has come to so many areas of the earth, where because of cynicism, indifference and falsity to democracy, we see now that saddest of all things in the human story, the epitaph of a vanished freedom.

And His Friends

O'Leary's gratitude to the great men in the march of parliamentary democracy was something which itself inspired respect. But if he worshipped his heroes, he cherished his friends no less: the taxi drivers (for he never drove a car), the golf and cribbage and poker players, the friends of his children, and the children of his friends. And, of course, his friends in politics. We earlier looked at his happiness in the company of two judges, let's look now at his words about three of his Senate colleagues.

When in 1963 T.A. Crerar returned to the Senate after some illness O'Leary in welcoming him back spoke of rich wisdom garnered from long years, "almost the lone survivor of a breed now all-but-extinct, that breed of Liberals who used to know what liberalism was about . . . I extend to him now that grand old Irish wish, that the good Lord may take a liking to him but not too soon." Hon. Norman Lambert, who died in 1966, "was for a stretch of almost fifty years my cherished friend. . . . He was a partisan but only because he had a deep faith in our party system, and he would never make a difference of opinion a cause for hatred."

O'Leary went on:

> There was one thing about Norman Lambert about which you could be absolutely sure: he would be closer to you in your hour of trial than in your hour of triumph. Almost every Sunday he would come to my home, and for an hour we would discuss old newspaper days, politics, of course, and books, poetry and literature—literature which he knew very well, the earthy worst and the heavenly best. He was a blunt man. He never courted popularity, and he never tried to bribe anybody into liking him by showing them only a part of himself . . . It was an unforgettable experience to hear and watch him miss a two foot putt. But, cheerfulness was always breaking through, and you knew that after his first moment of fury it would be followed by gales of laughter about himself. . . . A great son of Canada who loved and served Canada well, and one whose memory all of us in this house will keep until our own time has come.

That same year another "dear and tender friend for more than half a century" died—Senator Charles Gavan Power:

> When Senator Power published his book last year, he sent me a complimentary copy and on the flyleaf of it he wrote this: "To note the

remarkable fact that through fifty years of disagreement about almost everything, not an angry word ever passed between us—and we Irish, and Quebec Irish at that." I first met Senator Power when after World War I he returned as a minstrel boy and took his seat in the House of Commons, bursting on the floor of that chamber like a joyous firecracker and compelling the admiration and the affection of all. I always thought of him as one of the truly great speakers of the Parliament of Canada. He had wit, pathos, charm, and, most of all, he sometimes had that cadence of brooding Celtic melancholy reminiscent of the Great Timothy Healy who for long long years was a glory at Westminster. Chubby Power was human, God knows, but no man that I have known ever attoned more nobly for his humanity. I know that he had a disdain for what he called 'religiosity.' I know that he disdained the thoughtless meditation of saccharine piety, but he did have an abiding faith in God—he never believed that our world with all its cloud and pain, was all entanglement, dispersion and chaos, with no divine ordinance whatever. That is all I would say of Chubby Power . . . a very great Canadian, a very great human being has gone from us, and may God rest his soul.

Not a Sunday Christian

The reader has perhaps become aware that in a great variety of his speeches and writings Grattan O'Leary has touched on man's need of faith. Religion played a role in his daily life. He was not a Sunday Christian, often missed Mass, but the principles of justice, integrity, understanding, humility—and standing up for what seems right—were with him at work and play.

I remember his once holding the members of the Board of Trade transfixed by pausing to read the soft words of a hard economist John Maynard Keynes: "The day is coming, it may be overdue, when economics will have to be put in their proper place; when religion and morality will have to take priority, with more thought for things of the spirit—for justice, truth, and for love and beauty." I remember, too, being in the Senate Chamber when he stilled a debate on capital punishment by saying, not arrogantly but as in a confession: "Honorable senators, I cannot bring my conscience to believe that the state has any moral right, or any right whatsoever, to send a fellow human being to the judgment throne of God. This is not a power or right given to them.''

The Catholic Grattan O'Leary was Rector of the Scottish Presbyterian Queen's University. The Jews of Ottawa voted him Man of the Year. The Catholic Church newspaper *The Ensign* got from him the back of his hand for its narrowness. His library and mind were full of the great stories of the faiths of almost all men. He could sit with children or teenagers and smilingly remove their doubts, not by directive but by entering their minds with simple words and examples.

Yet though O'Leary's acceptance of another's concept of religion was respectful, he used to say in personal conversation that though Christ without the Cross was perhaps a decent way of life, it wasn't enough. In the fall of 1973 I asked him directly, ''What has religion meant and what does it mean to you?'' Here is his reply:

As a boy, religion meant a great deal to me, and in my sunset years it means still more to me. But I ask more questions. One cannot read the terrible story of what Christians have done to Christianity without wonder, perhaps without doubt, without a touch of agnosticism about some things accepted without question in youth. But here, again, it is a question of balance. A question of what the world would have been like if Christianity had not come to it. When I read Ranke's *Lives of the Popes*, I wondered. When I read Gibbon and Buckle's *History of Civilization*, I continued to wonder. But then I read Newman and Acton, and a lot of my faith was restored. Acton was critical of Rome, disagreed violently with some of its decrees. But when he was asked why he did not leave Rome, he replied: ''I disagree with what some of the temporary rulers of the Church say and do. But I often disagree and deplore what some of the temporary rulers of England say and do. That doesn't mean that I should resign as an Englishman. So what some temporary ruler may say or do in Rome need not mean that I resign from Rome.'' That can go for me. I may be dismayed by what has been done by Christians in the name of Christianity, but I balance that by what Christians have done for man's good. In ecumenism I do not believe, I cannot believe in unity of dogma. I do believe in unity of charity. If I believe in the last, and hate cruelty, injustice, intolerance, I am content to face the Unknown.

The Irish in Him

On a visit to Eire during the war O'Leary interviewed Premier de Valera in Dublin. ''Sir, before I begin, I want to say I haven't a drop of blood that isn't Irish.'' ''That's more than I can say,'' replied the Premier, ''my father was Spanish.''

Irish O'Leary was, for sure. I've talked about the Irish charm of him, let's tackle the Irish perversity, which I think he nourished for the fun and hell of it!

Sometimes at lunch with acquaintances (as distinct from close friends) the talk would turn to the issue of the day. Someone would give his view and Grattan would ask why he held that view—and keep asking until they seemed in violent dispute. Yet I knew Grattan had just that morning written an editorial for next day, along much the same line as our friend. He would explain to me later he was: (a) seeing whether the fellow knew anything; (b) exploring to see if he should change his editorial. Other times he'd do it to relieve a dull lunch!

In his maiden speech to the Senate, Oct. 17, 1962, he trumpeted: ''I am a Conservative, I am a party man.'' And he meant it.

Yet he also meant it when he'd flay the partisan party hacks. To the Senate he recalled Arthur Meighen telling him that when he was Conservative Leader in the Senate he met up one day with Senator Dandurand, the distinguished Government Leader. Meighen had said to him: ''I hope I will be a foeman worthy of your steel.'' Dandurand replied: ''You are wrong on two counts; you are not my foeman, and I am not worthy of your steel.'' O'Leary went on: ''That is what Dandurand believed, and that is what Meighen believed. And over the years Arthur Meighen was the leader of his party in this house, he never once attended a Conservative Party caucus, because, he said, he believed he should get that legislation cold when it came to him. And never once in all the years he was leader of the party in this house did R.B. Bennett, Conservative leader in the other place, ask Meighen to consult with him about legislation. He understood and Arthur Meighen understood, as Raoul Dandurand understood, what the Senate is really about.''

He explained to the bemused Senators what he meant. "Accepting the Conservative philosophy is to me a very different thing from accepting the Conservative party line. We are not here to accept the party line. We can have our political beliefs, but our sole responsibility is not to any party or Prime Minister that appointed us. Our sole responsibility here is to the people of Canada."

To the Davey Committee, speaking of his political writings, he exclaimed: "I was a maverick. I am glad I was. But I still believe in a party press."

When he thought it right to be a maverick and when to come to the aid of the party depended somewhat on his mood! One time the Senate Government leader Paul Martin said, "O'Leary is not usually as excited as he now obviously is." "I'm not cold about anything," he cried back. "I take sides and I do not cover up the sides I take by a lot of verbiage."

At Easter in 1964 he single-handedly refused to let the Senate approve tardily-presented and unexamined Government legislation on social security and unemployment insurance. He knew it would bring down on his head much public and political abuse, but after holding it up 36 hours, he said:

> I was myself a child of poverty, a child who was compelled to leave school before the age of twelve to gain a livelihood for himself and help gain a livelihood for his family. . . . If I felt (now) I had created hardship or sorrow or suffering I would indeed be sorry, but I would have the consolation of believing that perhaps a single day, or even two days, of a person's being deprived of social security or unemployment insurance is a very small price to pay for the assertion here of the rights of Parliament. . . . I will not again give consent if and when bills come to this house in future, and we are asked to suspend our rules in order to put the bills through to bail out the other place because of its incompetence and failure to manage its own business.

There was character in his standing up like that, and he did so often. "Hell hath no fury like an undelivered speech," he once said to the Senate. He would have been furious at himself if he had run away from the challenge of the Commons' trampling on Parliament's rights.

Granted, there were occasions when perhaps on an ill-sitting breakfast his spirit was sharper than his logic. And the opposition was quick then to needle him from bad to worse. But as his opponents were also his friends, they made their jibes urbanely. Paul Martin once intoned after an O'Leary attack on foreign policy: "I note all his arguments. I am sure he will not think I am disrespectful of him when I say that it can be shown clearly that they do not have the validity which his strong eloquence for the moment suggests." Liberal Senator Salter Hayden said it better: "Every time I have heard him speak—and I have heard him often, I am a great admirer—I have had to dig my feet firmly into the ground to keep from being carried away by the force and spell of his oratory." And his friend Senator Eugene Forsey: "I just could not help being struck by the series of eloquent contradictions in the speech of Senator O'Leary."

I'm sure Grattan knew he sometimes took a high road in pleading a cause. One time on being rebuked in the Senate for a rough attack he asked, almost meekly, "Is not anger the cleanest of passions?" But his anger was never nasty, rarely unkind; it was the theory he opposed, not the individual. It seemed to me sometimes that he did over-shoot, especially in foreign affairs. Perhaps he was irked by the mumbo-jumbo of diplomatic cover-up. I'm not sure he gave the same close reading to the texts and documents of UN and other international gatherings that he did to Canadian affairs, yet his criticism was just as vigorous. I'll give a few samples, though it is tearing single sentences out of context. "Do you know what I would do with NATO? I would get out of NATO lock, stock and barrel." "I do not think it matters very much if the Commonwealth, as constituted today, exists or not." "I submit to you that this (force in Cyprus) has never been a United Nations force: it has been a fraud on the people of this country (Canada) and on the world to call it a UN force." "Why did the Security Council intervene in the affairs of Rhodesia?" "We are running away with the nonsense that we (Canada) are a great country."

On hearing or reading those things I knew the particular sentences would have poured out in the course of an argument that would not have been so unqualified. I could imagine, too, the speech he would have made if someone had said Canada was *not* a great country, or that the Commonwealth was useless! To put it in a metaphor that would outrage the *New Yorker*, I think he often threw stones at sacred cows just to keep them on their toes. The man loved to praise and loved to argue. He had the gifts of mind, speech and temperament that enabled him to do both better than most anyone in our time. Had he gone to Oxford he'd have been able to take both sides of the case in the Debating Club and the eminent judges might have called it a draw—except that the case he voiced last would have won!

Let me illustrate. I have a faded piece of paper bearing his typing under the one-word title "Democracy":

> The truth is that the democratic theory saddles the individual citizen with an impossible task, and that he is asked to practise an unattainable ideal. I find it so myself. Although public business is my main interest and I give most of my time to watching it, I simply cannot find time to do what is expected of me by the democratic theory—that is, to know what is going on and to have an opinion worth expressing on every question which confronts a self-governing community. And I have not happened to meet anybody, from a Prime Minister of Canada to a professor of political science, who came anywhere near to embodying the accepted ideal of the sovereign and omnicompetent citizen. . . . And there isn't the least reason for thinking, as many mystical democrats have thought, that the compounding of individual ignorances in people can produce a safe directing force in public affairs.

That is all there was, and I don't know what he intended it for. I think it is about 30 years old. But now hear Michael Grattan as counsel for the defence, on another occasion:

> In this age when government reaches out into our very private lives it isn't easy for the average citizen to know all that is going on in government everywhere all the time. But what is possible is that we in this country try to build up a sort of pattern of public thought, a framework of public morality, a realization that democracy's chores are important. We must get our young people, above all, to realize that they have an individual personal responsibility for what goes on in their country, in their community. If we could achieve that much, and then try to select the best brains to represent us in our legislatures, in our parliament, and give them a decent chance to carry on the government of the country, I think that our democracy could be made to work. I

don't think it can be demonstrated that good government can come in any country unless it comes from the bottom, from the people themselves, from the people realizing that they have a responsibility.

Now Home to The Journal

Finally, from the great reach of his public interests, let me reclaim Grattan for *The Ottawa Journal*. He had been associate editor from 1932, exclusively involved in the editorial page but dedicated to all that Mr. Ross and my father meant the paper to be. When Ross died in 1949 Grattan became vice-president, still largely concerned with editorials. When my father died, Oct. 18, 1957, I naturally asked Grattan to become president. He urged instead that I take it, insisting he had little experience in general management problems and that his share ownership was much smaller than that of the Smith family—though Smith and O'Leary shares combined were only a minority. I convinced him that not only did the Smiths want him to be president but he would be the best man for the paper. "All right, but only until I am 75, the head of a newspaper should not be a day over 65." He was then the youngest 69 in the world. It was great news for everyone, particularly me.

Grattan at once brought his democratic sense of procedure to Board meetings and daily managment. Department heads were encouraged to state their views, not just on their own affairs but on the paper in general. Meetings were at once serious and humorous. Earnestly mistaken he could sometimes be, given to flights of idealism beyond the budget or the plant's efficiency, but he could abandon his argument with easy grace and vigorously push another's idea into performance. Revealingly, he used to delight to tell the story of Graham Towers appearing before a Commons committee. The governor of the Bank of Canada was asked why what he was now saying was the contrary of what he had told the committee five years earlier. "I was wrong," replied Towers, and that was that.

The Journal Joins a Group

Within two years of O'Leary's becoming president his realism, as great in some things as his idealism in others, enabled us to face an unpleasant fact: that the paper's financial strength was meagre, its plant outmoded and its opposition (the Southam chain) astute and well-heeled. I described earlier how P.D. Ross had subtly made known to me in 1946 that economic pressures would make it hard for *The Journal* to remain independent. Now, thirteen years later, that time had come. In April of 1959 the paper was sold to F.P. Publications. For the record, here is the story.

From before the war Ross and E.N.S. had discussed between themselves the possibility of sale, but they turned would-be buyers away until the need was critical. Some senior members of the staff had been able to buy some of Ross' shares at just under market price, but only by borrowing from the bank, which was marginal ownership. When Ross died, O'Leary and E.N.S. found themselves with a looming problem, and they too considered "offers"—but again put it off. That O'Leary himself had for some time worried about the future we have from him in a characteristically smiling way. In May 1956 he opened a serious address on economic affairs to a group of business people with an apology that he had become rusty as a speaker because "for the past year or two I have been trying to get out a newspaper by the grace of God and the Bank of Nova Scotia."

When my father died in October of 1957 succession duties made our group's holding of a minority of *The Journal* shares still more precarious. My family held less than a third of the shares, considerably on bank loan, whose maintenance depended on *Journal* dividends. O'Leary's shares and those of a few others similarly on bank loans were not enough to improve the position from rash to risky. Against a general slump or aggressive competition *The Journal* could disappear in a fire-sale. When an offer came from Victor Sifton of the Winnipeg *Free Press*, O'Leary and I decided we must explore it.

After our joint exploration of the offer, I asked O'Leary what he thought we should do. He said, softly, that in the light of the precarious nature of *The Journal*'s ownership "the most certain and perhaps the only way" to assure its continuity was to join a reputable man and paper like Victor Sifton and *The Free Press*. "Specially," Grattan added, "because they have put in writing that you and I will control its editorial policies so long as we are around, that its news and general policies will be maintained, and its staffers retained and given a pension plan we have not been able to afford."

I will not say I took his advice, for that would seem to be making Grattan responsible. On this I want to be immaculately correct. It was my own view, too. If there is blame, I share it fully; and that the rest of the Smith family agreed with the move was very much on my recommendation. In retrospect it is clear our problem was not unique. Seven strongly-owned independent papers have since 1959 found it necessary to join newspaper groups: *The Globe and Mail, La Presse* of Montreal, the Montreal *Gazette,* the Windsor *Star,* the Brantford *Expositor*, the Montreal *Star, Le Soleil* of Quebec—and the wealthy Toronto *Telegram* has died. But the far greater comfort is that *The Journal* remains alive, and all of its staffers have financial security they could not have known with us. I am glad, however, that Mr. Ross and my father did not have to do the deed; and I wish, for Grattan's sake, we had lasted out until he had gone—though to look at him now, he will outlast me!

Most sadly for us, and for Canadian journalism, Victor Sifton died suddenly two years after we had been together, on April 21, 1961. He was only 64. The FP group of newspapers which *The Journal* joined now embraces the Toronto *Globe*, the Winnipeg *Free Press*, the Vancouver *Sun*, the Victoria *Times*, the Victoria *Colonist*, the Lethbridge *Herald*, the Calgary *Albertan* and the Montreal *Star*. In that company *The Journal* can compete on fairer grounds with *The Ottawa Citizen*, which is a member of the Southam group that embraces the Hamilton *Spectator*, Montreal *Gazette*, Brantford *Expositor*, Windsor *Star*, Winnipeg *Tribune*, Calgary *Herald*, Edmonton *Journal*, Vancouver *Province*, Brandon *Sun*, Medicine Hat *News*, North Bay *Nugget*, Owen Sound *Times* and Prince George *Citizen*. The still greater evidence of the vulnerability of one-paper-ownership to today's economic pressures is growth of the Thomson Newspapers to 34 dailies, good newspapers with long service to their communities, but too hard pressed to go it alone.

In our early months of learning to run in a team rather than solo we all got a great lift from the companionship and still keen devotion of Grattan O'Leary. What he himself thought of it all was well put to the Senate Committee on Mass Media in 1970 when he was asked whether the growth of newspaper groups was a good thing. The important thing, he replied, was not whether a paper was owned by a group or individual but whether the group or the individual were good people, good publishers. He recalled that before we sold we had had earlier offers from individuals:

We had one man, I remember, and my friend Norman Smith will remember, who came in and put a cheque book on the table and said

"Fill it out." We wouldn't sell it. We didn't think he was a fit and proper person to run a paper like *The Journal* . . . We sold to people of character who had been in the newspaper business all their lives, understood the press and what it should be and what it stood for. I don't care if you call it a chain or not, we sold it to people. There is nothing to a newspaper but people. It is just like the Senate; there is nothing in the Senate but people.

Senator Fortier asked if O'Leary thought there was a trend toward group ownership of newspapers. Senator O'Leary replied:

This I think will depend a great deal on the financial and economic conditions. There is not a trend on the part of people but there is a compulsion. I would have liked, and I am sure my friend Norman Smith would have liked, to go on running *The Journal* as we were running it. We owned it, we were happy with it and we thought we knew what a newspaper should be. We thought that P.D. Ross and E. Norman Smith had a tradition in *The Journal* and they had. E. Norman Smith always said, we must go into a home with grace and courtesy and P.D. Ross used to tell me, "O'Leary, say what you like about a man's policies, but don't say anything about him personally that you wouldn't be prepared to say to him at your own dinner table." Now, that is the way to run a newspaper. That is why we refused to sell to certain people who wanted to buy *The Journal*, but that didn't apply to the Siftons. They were men of character. They were men who knew what a newspaper should be.

Himself to the Senate!
A happy and blessed event for all in *The Journal* came in September, 1962, when O'Leary was named to the Senate by Prime Minister Diefenbaker. We knew he would bring life and distinction to the Senate as he did to *The Journal*—but our own personal delight was even greater. We were warmed, too, by the things our colleagues in other papers wrote about him. "A Senator Indeed!" said the Montreal *Gazette*: "He has proved that a man may fight for his party and lose nothing of his magnanimity: that he may have strong convictions and yet not harden into narrowness." The Hamilton

Spectator put in neatly: "This bright and learned gentleman will awaken the Senate." Our immediate opposition, *The Ottawa Citizen*, did it with high grace: "A man who has adorned the world of journalism and the public life of Canada for more than half a century . . . the kind of man the Senate needs."

O'Leary had instructed me he wanted nothing in *The Journal* about his going to the Senate except the plain news story; but over the years his Irish contrariness has rubbed off on me somewhat. About a week later I did a signed piece on the editorial page of which he knew nothing until the paper hit his doorstep Saturday noon. After quoting from many of the outside editorials on him I asked whether his friends at *The Journal* might not get a word in edgewise. About him as a Senator I said, in part:

There have been whispers that Mr. O'Leary is a Tory! If breadth of thought, tolerance and willingness to adventure are the marks of liberalism he is more liberal than any Liberal we can think of in politics today. But if Tory principles imply, as Lord Hailsham said of Conservatives not long ago, that "We are tenders of a garden, not curators of a museum," then Mr. O'Leary is a Tory.

Once, quite without warning, I asked him what Conservatism was. He sat still for maybe 15 seconds, looking out the window, and then replied with an opinion as rounded as though it had been polished for a week, "Conservative philosophy does not take up unreconnoitred ground with risk of disastrous defeat, does not adapt policies to the future without reference to the past, relates experiment always to experience."

So it's to the Senate! That body needn't fear he'll raise Hell or make a circus out of it—nobody can be more earnestly heedful than he of the dignity of Parliament and the restraints which stand between free speech and licence. He'll do it proud and try to be useful.

"God bless all in this House," he'll say to himself as he walks in to the debates—but though he'll be gentle with most of its foibles we don't recommend to the old tenants, Liberal or Tory, any demonstration of untruth, pomposity or laziness. He's sheer delight when they show up anywhere and, for all its grandeur, he'll be no different in the Senate.

But happy though we were, his going to the Senate gave me a problem. He wrote me that he felt it would be "unfair to the paper" for him to remain as president or editor, now that he was to be "actively associated" with the Government's political campaign. I replied that I wished to God he would retain both positions, that I knew him too well to think his being a Senator would prejudice the judgment he would bring to *The Journal*. He wouldn't yield, reminding me he had said in 1957 he thought no editor should be more than 65 and he was now approaching 75. He wanted to retire both jobs by year-end. I wrote him still again, and took it to his house on a Sunday. Monday he dropped on my desk a note in the green ink he always used. It is a bit personal but it shows so much of the man:

> Dear Norman: I can't leave the office today without at least acknowledging your note, not only for its generosity but for its cogency. I shall think about all you say, and long. Grattan.

We neither of us raised the subject again for several months. On Dec. 27 I received Grattan's resignation in writing for Jan. 1, from both posts! But I did talk him into retaining the presidency, and when he said he would insist on turning that over in April of 1963, three months hence, I chose to ignore it. On January 2, 1963, our leading editorial bore the title "This Newspaper—and Its Editors." It tells something of what we all thought of him then, and still do. It said, in part:

> Not easily to any typewriter in this building come the words Grattan O'Leary has retired the editorship of this newspaper. By remaining President and Editor Emeritus, he enables his colleagues (and pupils) in the office to moderate a little the sense of aloneness and responsibility that is theirs today . . . If many of our readers are wondering what the editorial page will be like without Grattan O'Leary, we here may add only that their wonder is nothing compared to our own. Certainly their sense of personal loss is nothing to ours. . . . Yet we are not quite alone. There is, we are aware, a *Journal* tradition, a *Journal* "way." From these traditions, from P.D. Ross and E. Norman Smith as from Grattan O'Leary, we who follow on have gained, let us hope, some degree of

what it is that readers have come to expect from this paper . . . The new editor and his two associate editors, Mr. James McCook and Dr. John W. Grace, say only that we will do our best, for not the least of the things Grattan O'Leary and the others have nourished in us is a genuine love of the task and a profound sense of its importance.

He "Retires"

Three years and three months later, on March 23, 1966, Senator O'Leary's firm smiling face looked out from a *Journal* news story announcing his retirement as president. He was 78. He was persuaded to retain the title of Editor Emeritus, but though grateful for it he said he never quite knew what it meant and believed the people in the daily run of the paper's work should bear the titles as well as the heat—"not retired old men." He said a week later to *Time* magazine: "Last year they persuaded me to stay, but this year I said 'Now look, I am going. I shouldn't be here at 78.' " We clung on, though, fitting out his old office a few yards along the hall with his trusty typewriter, the cigarette-charred typewriter-stand and his books and pictures. My colleagues Jim McCook, John Grace, Bruce Yemen and the secretary, Claudette Beaulieu, marched in and sang him a song-o that "apart from the fact that you'll be in a different room we regard nothing as having changed." Actually, he wrote almost nothing after retiring, rarely even suggested things; for he was determined not to "interfere." Gradually his visits became less frequent, for now his Senate office was where the action was. But we'd see him from time to time, in to look up a file or get out of the rain, as he put it. His heart was still in the place. Only in 1971 when the paper moved to what he in his Irish way called "modren" quarters, did he ask to be excused. "I'd not feel at home in that palatial new building, Norman," a slightly critical and very nostalgic look in his eye. I understood.

The day he retired as President he had left me yet another of those notes that show how thoughtful he always was of others, how sensitive to "occasions." I hope my quoting it is not too immodest.

Dear Norman:

I must say I appreciate your trying to make this change for me as little disturbing as possible. It is what I wanted—and *want*. *You* to be

President, and I feeling that *The Journal* will be in good hands that way.

A bit of a break I will feel, no doubt, when I walk out of here next Thursday, but there is no sense in making it more than it is, and it will be nothing to other changes that have come to me this year. [Mrs. O'Leary had died just six months earlier.]

Certainly I don't feel like crying, and if I did I always try to remember the good saying (actually by an old Irish Fenian with the name of John O'Leary) that one must never cry in public.

Thanks, Norman, for everything, and I hope that always while I am around I'll be at your back with anything I can do for you.

Grattan

He was, and he did.

How did he take "retirement"? He didn't retire. He had no seeming awareness that he was 78. He simply transferred his caring and energies to the Senate and to politics, and to putting all he had into life and friendships. For him the Senate would be no wax museum. The last sentence of an editorial I wrote on his 81st birthday will serve better than anything I can write now as a kind of farewell:

Michael Grattan O'Leary will have no part of asking the world to stop so he can get off. He likes it here and plans to go on affectionately belting the living daylights out of anyone who isn't carrying a share of the load with good cheer. We don't see Grattan around this building much now, more's the pity, but we can still "feel" him—and rue the day when this newspaper ceases to "feel" him, though it be a hundred years from now.

In the Spring of 1974 I add only this: Grattan is 86, "too old to be a pessimist," alight with interest and caring for "all in this house"—his house being all Canada, and beyond.